DEMOCRACY
ANCIENT AND
MODERN

Other books by M. I. Finley

STUDIES IN LAND AND CREDIT IN ANCIENT ATHENS, 1952, 1985

THE WORLD OF ODYSSEUS, 1954, 1977

THE ANCIENT GREEKS, 1963

ASPECTS OF ANTIQUITY, 1968

ANCIENT SICILY, 1968, 1979

EARLY GREECE, 1970, 1981

THE ANCIENT ECONOMY, 1973, 1985

THE USE AND ABUSE OF HISTORY, 1975

THE OLYMPIC GAMES—THE FIRST THOUSAND YEARS, 1976

ANCIENT SLAVERY AND MODERN IDEOLOGY, 1980

ECONOMY AND SOCIETY IN ANCIENT GREECE, 1981

POLITICS IN THE ANCIENT WORLD, 1983

ANCIENT HISTORY: EVIDENCE AND MODELS, 1985

DEMOCRACY
ANCIENT AND
MODERN

BY M. I. FINLEY

Revised Edition

 RUTGERS UNIVERSITY PRESS
New Brunswick and London

Library of Congress Cataloging in Publication Data

Finley, M. I. (Moses I.), 1912–
    Democracy ancient and modern.

    (Mason Welch Gross lectureship series)
    Includes bibliographies and index.
    1. Athens (Greece)—Politics and government—
Addresses, essays, lectures. 2. Democracy—History—
Addresses, essays, lectures. I. Title. II. Series.
JC79.A8F5 1985   320.938′5   85–2115
ISBN 0–8135–1126–7
ISBN 0–8135–1127–5 (pbk.)

To
My Friends and Students
at Rutgers University,
1948–52

Contents

PREFACE   ix

PREFACE TO THE FIRST EDITION   xi

1   LEADERS AND FOLLOWERS   3

2   ATHENIAN DEMAGOGUES   38

3   DEMOCRACY, CONSENSUS AND THE NATIONAL
INTEREST   76

4   SOCRATES AND AFTER   110

5   CENSORSHIP IN CLASSICAL ANTIQUITY   142

NOTES   173

INDEX   187

Preface

In the western world today everyone is a democrat. That is a remarkable change from the situation prevailing one hundred and fifty years ago, made possible in part by a drastic reduction in the element of popular participation that had been present in the original Greek conception of democracy, and helped ideologically by the spread of a theory justifying that reduction. The elitist theory, as it is commonly called, holds that democracy can function and survive only under a *de facto* oligarchy of professional politicians and bureaucrats; that popular participation must be restricted to occasional elections; that, in other words, popular political apathy is a good thing, a sign of health in the society.

The lectures I gave in the United States in 1972, which provided the core of this book, were expressly designed to combat the elitist theory. As I said in the original preface, I write as a professional histo-

rian, not as a political scientist or theorist. I tried
to develop a dialectical discourse between the ancient
Greek and the modern conceptions, within the limits
that are possible in discussing two such radically different worlds, in the belief that each society can help
us to understand the other. Not everyone has com-
prehended what I was trying to do, and some have
wholly misunderstood (as pointed out by my friend
Carmine Ampolo in the postface he wrote for the second Italian edition). I remain firm in my faith in this
kind of discourse. In the present edition, I have
added two previously published essays that I hope will
clarify as well as elaborate my thinking. I have also
made a number of small corrections and have added a
few more recent references to the notes.

M.I.F.

Darwin College, Cambridge
November 1984

Preface
to the First Edition

This book is the text, substantially unaltered though slightly enlarged, revised and annotated, of the three lectures I gave in New Brunswick in April, as the first of the Mason Welch Gross Lectures. The theme, and in a way the manner, reflect the occasion: it seemed to me appropriate that I should speak professionally, as an ancient historian, but at the same time bring the ancient (Greek) experience to bear on the subject of a major contemporary discussion, the theory of democracy. This kind of discourse, once not uncommon, has fallen into desuetude. The interest shown by the Rutgers audience, at least, suggests that I am not wrong in thinking that it is a legitimate, even fruitful, kind of discourse.

The opportunity I was given to initiate this new lecture series was an unexpected and most welcome honour, above all because it permitted me to share in a tribute to Mason Gross, whom I have known and admired for many years (and who is a member of my Cambridge College). The eight days my wife and I spent in New Brunswick and Newark, after an absence of twenty years, could not possibly be surpassed in warmth and friendliness. I trust I shall be forgiven if I single out for particular thanks our hosts, Dick and Suzanne Schlatter in New Brunswick, Horace De Podwin in Newark, and do not go on to name the other old friends and former students who contributed to the festivity.

I must also express my gratitude to my friend and colleague, Quentin Skinner of Christ's College, for his invaluable counsel at several stages in the preparation of this book; and, as with all my books, to the help of my wife.

M.I.F.

Jesus College, Cambridge
July 24, 1972

DEMOCRACY
ANCIENT AND
MODERN

1 *Leaders and Followers*

Perhaps the best known, and certainly the most vaunted, "discovery" of modern public opinion research is the indifference and ignorance of a majority of the electorate in western democracies.* They cannot state the issues, about most of which they do not care anyway; many do not know what the Common Market is, or even the United Nations; many cannot name their representatives or who is running for which office. Appeals for a public lobbying campaign, if they are sensible, always carry some such notice as the following: "Your public library can tell you the names of your Senators and Representatives if you aren't sure of them." [1] In some countries, a majority do not even bother to exercise their treasured right to vote.

At issue is not only the descriptive question of how democracy functions but also the prescriptive or normative one of what, if anything, ought to be done about it. There is a large and growing body of learned

---

* I write "discovery" in inverted commas because the phenomenon was already well known to older political analysts.

discussion on the subject, some of which has a slight echo effect to the historian of antiquity. When Seymour Martin Lipset writes that extremist movements "appeal to the disgruntled and the psychologically homeless, to the personal failures, the socially isolated, the economically insecure, the uneducated, unsophisticated, and authoritarian persons at every level of society," [2] the stress on the uneducated and the unsophisticated awakens echoes of Plato's persistent objection to the role of shoemakers and shopkeepers in political decision-making. Or when Aristotle (*Politics*, 1319a19-38) argued that the best democracy will be in a state with a large rural hinterland and a relatively numerous population of farmers and herdsmen, who "are scattered over the country, do not meet together so often or feel the need of assembling," one feels a kinship with a contemporary political scientist, W. H. Morris Jones, who wrote, in an article with the revealing title, "In Defence of Apathy," that "many of the ideas connected with the general theme of a Duty to Vote belong properly to the totalitarian camp and are out of place in the vocabulary of liberal democracy"; that political apathy is a "sign of understanding and tolerance of human variety" and has a "beneficial effect on the tone of political life" because it is a "more or less effective counter-force to the fanatics who constitute the real danger to liberal democracy." [3]

I am not, I hasten to add, about to embark on the

banal theme, there is nothing new under the sun. Professor Lipset would be astonished, and probably horrified, to be called a Platonist, and I doubt that Professor Morris Jones thinks of himself as an Aristotelian. To begin with, Plato and Aristotle both disapproved of democracy in principle, whereas the two modern critics are democrats. Furthermore, whereas all ancient political theorists examined the different forms of government normatively, that is to say, by their ability to help man achieve a moral goal in society, justice and the good life, modern writers who share the orientation of Lipset and Morris Jones are less ambitious: they avoid ideal goals, concepts such as the good life, and they stress the means, the efficiency of the political system, its peacefulness and openness.

A powerful impetus to the new view was provided by the publication in 1942 of Joseph Schumpeter's *Capitalism, Socialism, and Democracy,* in which one of the critical steps is "that he defines democracy as a *method* which is well designed to produce a strong, authoritative government. No ideals are attached to the definition of a democracy itself. It does not in itself imply any notions of civic responsibility or of widespread political participation, or any ideas of the ends of man. . . . Liberty and equality which have been part and parcel of past definitions of democracy are regarded by Schumpeter as not being integral parts of such a definition, however worthy they may be as ideals." [4]

Plato's kind of goal is therefore rejected not only as the wrong goal but, more radically, because it is a goal. Ideal goals are a menace in themselves, as much in more modern philosophies as in Plato. Sir Karl Popper's *The Open Society and Its Enemies* is perhaps the best known expression of such a view, but it is equally present (though he would probably deny the association) in Sir Isaiah Berlin's distinction between the "negative" and "positive" concepts of liberty, between freedom from interference and coercion, which is a good thing, and freedom to achieve self-realization which, history shows, according to Sir Isaiah, easily slides into a justification of "the coercion of some men by others in order to raise them to a 'higher' level of freedom," a "sleight of hand" performed once it was decided that "freedom as rational self-direction . . . applied not merely to a man's inner life, but to his relations with other members of his society." [5]

There is another way to appreciate the fundamental difference in point of view. Both Plato and Lipset would leave politics to experts, the former to rigorously trained philosophers who, having apprehended the Truth, will thereafter be guided by the Truth absolutely; the latter to professional politicians (or to politicians in consort with the bureaucracy), who will be guided by their expertise in the art of the possible and be periodically checked by an election, the democratic device that gives the people a choice between competing groups of experts, and, to that extent, a measure of control. Although both agree that popular *initiative* in political decisions is disastrous—that "government of the people, by the people, and for the people" is naive ideology—the divergence reflected in the distinction between the two different kinds of expert expresses two fundamentally different views of the goal of politics, different views of the ends that the state should serve. Plato was totally opposed to popular government; Lipset favours it provided there is more "government" (as distinct from tyranny or anarchy) in the mixture than "popular," in particular provided that there is no popular *participation* in the classic sense. Hence "apathy" is transformed into a political good, a virtue, one which, in some mysterious way overcomes itself (and the underlying political ignorance) in those occasional moments when the people are invited to choose among competing groups of experts.[6]

I might have said "an elite" rather than experts. Elitist theories of politics and of democracy have become familiar on the academic scene, though less so, for obvious public relations reasons, among practising politicians, ever since the conservative Mosca and Pareto introduced them in Italy at the turn of the present century, followed by the even more influential work of Robert Michels, *Political Parties*, published

shortly before the first world war.[7] The latter, then a
German Social Democrat (though later an enthusiastic
supporter of Mussolini, at whose personal invitation
he took a chair at the University of Perugia in 1928),
was politically and psychologically hostile to elites,
and preferred the word "oligarchy": the subtitle of his
book is "A Sociological Study of the Oligarchical Tendencies of Modern Democracy."

There are semantic difficulties with the word "elite."
It has always had, and still retains, too wide a range
of meanings, many of them irrelevant or misleading in
the present context, the traditional aristocratic sense,
for example.[8] Some of the most influential political scientists for whom Lipset has been my symbol find the
elitist label offensive (though not Lipset himself).[9]
Despite these objections—and I confess to being un-
moved by the indignation—"elitist theory of democracy" identifies the view more aptly than any other
proposed label, and I shall use it henceforth.

Labels apart, there is clearly a major historical problem to be examined, a problem in both the history of
ideas and the history of politics at one and the same
time. In antiquity, intellectuals in the overwhelming
majority disapproved of popular government, and they
produced a variety of explanations for their attitude
and a variety of alternative proposals. Today their
counterparts, especially but not only in the west, are
agreed, in probably the same overwhelming majority,

that democracy is the best form of government, the best known and the best imaginable; yet many are also agreed that the principles on which democracy had traditionally been justified are not operating in practice; furthermore, that they cannot be allowed to operate if democracy is to survive. Ironically, the elitist theory is being pressed with particular vigour in Britain and the United States, empirically the two most successful democracies of modern times. How did we reach this curious, paradoxical position?

That there is a semantic confusion in the position is obvious. "Democracy" and "democratic," one analyst has recently observed, "have become in the twentieth century words which imply approval of the society or institution so described. This has necessarily meant that the words have become debased in that they have almost ceased without further definition to be of any use in distinguishing one particular form of government from another." [10] However, semantic change is never accidental or socially indifferent. It has not often been the case in the past that use of the word "democracy" automatically "implied approval of the society or institution so described." In antiquity it was equally a word whose use by many writers implied strong disapproval. Then the word disappeared from the popular vocabulary until the eighteenth century, when it crept back as a pejorative term. "It is rare, even among the *philosophes* of France before the Revolution, to find anyone using the word 'democracy' in a favourable sense in any practical connection." [11] When Wordsworth wrote in a private letter in 1794, "I am of that odious class of men called 'democrats,' " [12] he was being defiant, not satirical.

The American and French revolutions then initiated the great nineteenth-century debate, which ultimately ended with total victory for one side. In the United States in the thirties of the present century, to be sure, there were still voices who proclaimed that the Founding Fathers never intended a democracy, but a republic; however, they were, and are, fairly insignificant. Huey Long caught the correct tone when he said that, if fascism came to the United States, it would arrive in the name of antifascism. Popular support for McCarthy "represented less a conscious rejection of American democratic ideals than a misguided effort to defend them." [13]

From one point of view, this consensus amounts to a debasement of the concept to the point of analytical uselessness, as we have seen. However, it would be a mistake to leave the matter at that. If such bitter opponents as the academic advocates of the elitist theory and the student advocates of the demonstration and the continuous mass meeting both claim to be defending real or genuine democracy, we are witnessing a new phenomenon in human history, the novelty and significance of which deserve underscoring. We must consider not only why the classical theory of democracy appears to be in contradiction with the observed practice, but also why the many different responses to this observation, though mutually incompatible, all share the belief that democracy is the best form of political organization.

The historical aspect of this situation is receiving less attention than it merits. It is not self-evident, I submit, that there should now be such near unanimity about the virtue of democracy when during most of history the reverse was the case. To dismiss this unanimity as a debasement of the currency, or to dismiss the other side of the debate as ideologists who misuse the term, is to evade the need for explanation. The history of ideas is never just the history of ideas; it is also the history of institutions, of society itself. Michels thought he had discovered an "iron law of oligarchy"—"Democracy leads to oligarchy, and necessarily contains an oligarchical nucleus. . . . The law that is an essential characteristic of all human aggregates to constitute cliques and sub-cliques is, like every other sociological law, beyond good and evil." [14] The conclusion left him with a deep pessimism (until his conversion to Mussolini). [15]

More recent "elitists" have tried to remove the stigma. There is a fault in Michels' "definition," they say, when he characterizes *any separation* between leaders and followers as *ipso facto* a negation of democracy." [16]

Empirical observation, they continue, reveals that this separation between leaders and followers is operationally universal in democracies, and, since everyone agrees that democracy is the best form of government, it follows that the empirically observed "separation" is a quality, not a negation, of democracy, and therefore a virtue. "The distinctive and *most valuable* element of democracy is the formation of a political elite in the competitive struggle for the votes of a mainly passive electorate" (my italics).[17] This apparent syllogism entails "one false and ideological move," an attempt to redescribe a given and *prima facie* untoward state of affairs in such a way as to legitimate it.[18] No argument is offered, other than the warm glow evoked by the word "democracy," to justify current procedures in western democracies. They are simply approved by definition, as a counter to Michels' "oligarchic" definition.

It is precisely at this point that an historical consideration may be useful, specifically a consideration of the ancient Greek experience. "Democracy" is of course a Greek word. The second half of the word means "power" or "rule," hence autocracy is rule by one man; aristocracy, rule by the *aristoi*, the best people, the elite; democracy, rule by the *demos*, the people. *Demos* was a Protean word with several meanings, among them "the people as a whole" (or the citizen-body to be more precise) and "the common people" (the lower classes), and the ancient theoretical debates often played with this central ambiguity. As usual, it was Aristotle who produced the most penetrating socio-logical formulation (*Politics*, 1279b34-80a4): "The argument seems to show that the number of the governing body, whether small in an oligarchy or large in a democracy, is an accident due to the fact that the rich everywhere are few, and the poor numerous. Therefore . . . the real difference between democracy and oligarchy is poverty and wealth. Wherever men rule by reason of their wealth, whether they be few or many, that is an oligarchy, and where the poor rule, that is a democracy."

Aristotle's point was not merely descriptive. Behind his taxonomy lay a normative distinction, between rule in the general interest, the sign of a better type of government, and rule in the interest of, for the benefit of, a particular section of the population, the mark of a worse type. The danger inherent in democracy, for Aristotle, was then that rule by the poor would deteriorate into rule in the interest of the poor, a view that will concern us in chapters 2 and 3. Here I shall concentrate on the more narrowly instrumental question of the relationship between leaders and followers in policy-making.

It was the Greeks, after all, who discovered not only democracy but also politics, the art of reaching decisions by public discussion and then of obeying those decisions as a necessary condition of civilized social existence. I am not concerned to deny the possibility that there were prior examples of democracy, so-called tribal democracies, for instance, or the democracies in early Mesopotamia that some Assyriologists believe they can trace. Whatever the facts may be about the latter, their impact on history, on later societies, was null. The Greeks, and only the Greeks, discovered democracy in that sense, precisely as Christopher Columbus, not some Viking seaman, discovered America.

The Greeks were then—and this no one will dispute—the first to think systematically about politics, to observe, describe, comment and eventually to formulate political theories. For good and sufficient reason, the only Greek democracy we are able to study in depth, that of Athens in the fifth and fourth centuries B.C., was also the most seminal one intellectually. It was Greek writing provoked by the Athenian experience that the eighteenth and nineteenth centuries read, insofar as reading history played a role in the rise and development of modern democratic theories. It is therefore Athens that we shall be considering when we discuss ancient democracy.*

---

* The Romans discussed democracy, too, but what they had to say has little interest. It was derivative in the worst sense, derivative from books alone, since Rome itself was never a democracy by any acceptable definition of that term, though popular institutions were incorporated into the oligarchic governmental system of the Roman Republic.

So strong was the Athenian impact that even some contemporary elitist theorists make their bow to it, if only to pronounce it no longer relevant. Two of the reasons frequently adduced have less weight than claimed. One is the argument from the greater complexity of modern governmental activity; the fallacy is that problems arising from international monetary agreements or space satellites are technical problems, not political ones, "capable of being settled by experts or machines like arguments between engineers or doctors." [19] Athens employed financial and engineering experts, too, and the undeniably greater simplicity of their technical problems does not of itself imply a comparably great political difference in the two situations. Technical, and especially military, experts have always exercised an influence, and have always tried to extend that influence, but political decisions are made by political leaders, today as in the past. The "managerial revolution" has not altered that fundamental fact of political life.[20]

Then there is the argument from slavery: the Athenian *demos* was a minority elite from which a large slave population was totally excluded. True, and the presence of numerous slaves could not fail to have affected both practice and ideology. It fostered an openness, a frankness, about exploitation, for example, and one justification for war, both together expressed bluntly by Aristotle when (*Politics*, 1333b38-34a1) he included among the reasons why statesmen must know the art of warfare, "in order to become masters of those who deserve to be enslaved." On the other hand, an account of the social structure of Athens is far from exhausted by this binary division into free men and slaves. Before we accept that the elitism of the *demos* renders their experience irrelevant to ours, we must examine more closely the composition of that elite minority, the *demos*, the citizenry.

A common view was stated this way half a century ago: "By general elementary education we have begun to teach the art of manipulating ideas to those who in Ancient Society were slaves. . . . Half-educated people are in a very susceptible condition, and the world today consists mainly of half-educated people. They are capable of seizing ideas, but they have not attained to the habit of testing them and of suspense of mind in the meantime." [21] If that is a valid proposition about the half-educated—I do not discuss that—its political application in ancient Athens was not to the slaves but to a large section of the *demos*, to the peasants, shopkeepers and craftsmen who were citizens alongside the educated upper classes. The incorporation of such people into the political community as full members, an astounding novelty in its time, rarely repeated thereafter, rescues some of the relevance of ancient democracy, so to speak.

The Athenian population occupied a territory of

about one thousand square miles, roughly equal to Derbyshire, Rhode Island or the Duchy of Luxemburg. At no time in the fifth and fourth centuries B.C. did more than half of them live in the two urban centres, the city of Athens and the harbour-town, the Piraeus; for most of the fifth century, in fact, the urban fraction was probably nearer one third than one half. The others lived in villages, such as Acharnae, Marathon and Eleusis, not on homestead-farms, which were always, and still are, rare in the Mediterranean. One third or one half of how many? No precise figures are available, but it is a fair guess that the adult male citizens never exceeded thirty-five or forty thousand, and dropped well below that total at times, for example when Athens was decimated by plague in the years 430 to 426 B.C. With such small numbers, concentrated in small residential groupings and living the typically Mediterranean out-of-doors life, ancient Athens was the model of a face-to-face society, familiar to us in a university community perhaps but now unknown on a municipal scale, let alone a national scale.[22] "A state composed of too many," Aristotle wrote in a famous passage (*Politics*, 1326b3-7), "will not be a true state, for the simple reason that it can hardly have a true constitution. Who can be the general of a mass so excessively large? And who can be herald, except Stentor?"

The reference to the herald (the town crier) is illuminating. The Greek world was primarily one of the

spoken, not the written, word. Information about public affairs was chiefly disseminated by the herald, the
notice board, gossip and rumour, verbal reports and
discussions in the various commissions and assemblies
that made up the governmental machinery. This was a
world not only without mass media but without media
at all, in our sense. Political leaders, lacking documents
that could be kept secret (apart from the occasional
exception), lacking media they could control, were of
necessity brought into a direct and immediate relationship with their constituents, and therefore under more
direct and immediate control. I do not say that in
Athens there was no possibility of what it is now
fashionable to express in the euphemism, credibility
gap, but that if it arose it would have been a different
kind of gap, with a different force.

Differences in public communication are of course
not a sufficient explanation. There was a more weighty
factor: Athenian democracy was direct, not representative, in a double sense; attendance in the sovereign
Assembly was open to every citizen, and there was no
bureaucracy or civil service, save for a few clerks, slaves
owned by the state itself, who kept such records as
were unavoidable, copies of treaties and laws, lists of
defaulting taxpayers, and the like. Government was
thus "by the people" in the most literal sense. The Assembly, which had the final decision on war and peace,
treaties, finance, legislation, public works, in short, on

the whole gamut of governmental activity, was an outdoor mass meeting of as many thousand citizens, over
the age of eighteen, as chose to attend on any given
day. It met frequently throughout the year, forty times
at a minimum, and it normally reached a decision on
the business before it in a single day's debate in which,
in principle, everyone present had the right to partici-
pate by taking the floor. *Isegoria,* the universal right
to speak in the Assembly, was sometimes employed by
Greek writers as a synonym for "democracy." And the
decision was by a simple majority vote of those present.

The administrative side of government was divided
among a large number of annual offices and a Council
of 500, all chosen by lot and restricted to one or two
one-year terms, with the exception of the board of ten
generals and such small *ad hoc* commissions as em-
bassies to another state. By the middle of the fifth century B.C., officeholders, Council members and jurors
were paid a small *per diem,* less than a normal day's
pay for a skilled mason or carpenter. Early in the fourth
century, attendance at the Assembly was paid on the
same basis, though in this case there is doubt about
either the regularity of the pay or the completeness.[23]
Selection by lot and pay for office were the linchpin of
the system. Elections, said Aristotle (*Politics,* 1300b4-5),
are aristocratic, not democratic: they introduce the
element of deliberate choice, of selection of the "best

people," the *aristoi,* in place of government by all the people.

A considerable proportion of the male citizens of Athens therefore had some direct experience in government beyond anything we know, almost beyond anything we can imagine. It was literally true that at birth every Athenian boy had better than a gambler's chance to be president of the Assembly, a rotating post held for a single day and, as always, filled by the drawing of lots. He might be a market commissioner for a year, a member of the Council for one year or two (though not in succession), a juryman repeatedly, a voting member of the Assembly as frequently as he liked. Behind this direct experience, to which should be added the administration of the hundred-odd parishes or "demes" into which Athens was subdivided, there was also the general familiarity with public affairs that even the apathetic could not escape in such a small, face-to-face society.

Hence the question of the educational level and knowledge of the average citizen, so important in our current debates about democracy, had a different dimension in Athens. In formal terms, most Athenians were no better than "half-educated," and Plato was not the only ancient critic to hammer the point. When in the winter of 415 B.C. the Assembly voted *nem. con.* to send a great expeditionary force to Sicily, they were, says the historian Thucydides (6.1.1) with an unconcealed sneer, "for the most part ignorant of the size of the island or of the number of its inhabitants." Even if that were true, Thucydides was making the mistake, already noted, of confusing technical knowledge and political understanding. There were enough experts in Athens to advise the Assembly on the size and population of Sicily and on the scale of the armada that would be required. Thucydides himself conceded, in a later chapter of his *History* (6.31), that the expedition was in the end thoroughly prepared and fully equipped; that, too, I may add, was the work of experts, the Assembly's role being limited to accepting their advice and voting the necessary financing and troop mobilization.

The practical decisions were taken at a second meeting of the Assembly several days after the invasion of Sicily had been decided in principle. Again Thucydides allowed himself a personal comment on the final vote (6.24.3-4): "There was a passion for the expedition which seized everyone alike. The older men thought that they would either conquer the places against which they were sailing or, in any case, with such a large force, could come to no harm; the young had a longing for the sights and experiences, and were confident that they would return safely; the mass of the people, including the soldiers, saw the prospect of earning money for the time being, and by adding to the empire, of assuring income in the future. The result of this excessive enthusiasm of the great majority was that those who actually were opposed to the expedition were afraid of being thought unpatriotic if they voted against it, and therefore kept quiet."

It would be easy to preach about the irrationality of crowd behaviour at an open-air mass meeting, swayed by demagogic orators, chauvinistic patriotism and so on. But it would be a mistake to overlook that the vote in the Assembly to invade Sicily had been preceded by a period of intense discussion, in the shops and taverns, in the town square, at the dinner table— a discussion among the same men who finally came together on the Pnyx for the formal debate and vote. There could not have been a man sitting in the Assembly that day who did not know personally, and often intimately, a considerable number of his fellow-voters, his fellow-members of the Assembly, including perhaps some of the speakers in the debate. Nothing could be more unlike the situation today, when the individual citizen from time to time engages, along with *millions* of others, not just a few thousand of his neighbours, in the impersonal act of marking a ballot-paper or manipulating the levers of a voting-machine. Moreover, as Thucydides said explicitly, many were voting that day to take themselves off on campaign, in the army or the navy. Listening to a political debate with that end in view would have focussed the minds of the participants clearly and sharply. It would have given the debate a reality and spontaneity that modern parliaments may once have had but now notoriously lack.

It might therefore appear that the lack of interest in Athenian democracy by contemporary political scientists is justified. Certainly there is nothing to be learned on the constitutional side; the requirements and the rules of the ancient Greek system are simply irrelevant. However, constitutional history is a surface phenomenon. Much of the rich political history of the United States in the twentieth century lies outside the sphere of the "civics" I had to study as a schoolboy. And of ancient Athens, too.

Under the governmental system I have described briefly, Athens managed for nearly two hundred years to be the most prosperous, most powerful, most stable, most peaceful internally, and culturally by far the richest state in all the Greek world. The system worked, insofar as that is a useful judgment about any form of government. "As for the Athenian system of government," wrote an oligarchic pamphleteer of the latter part of the fifth century B.C. (Ps.-Xenophon, *Constitution of Athens*, 3.1), "I do not like it. However, since they decided to become a democracy, it seems to me that they are preserving the democracy well." Even though the Assembly voted to invade an island of which they knew neither the size nor the population, the system worked.

"Neither is poverty a bar," Pericles is reported to

have said in a speech commemorating the war dead
(Thucydides, 2.37.1), "but a man may benefit his *polis*
whatever the obscurity of his condition." Widespread
public participation in the affairs of the state, including
"the personal failures, the socially isolated, the economically insecure, the uneducated," did not lead to
"extremist movements." The evidence is that few actually exercised the right to speak in the Assembly, which
did not suffer fools; it acknowledged, in its behaviour,
the existence of political as well as technical expertise,
and it looked to a few men in any given period to lay
down alternative policy lines from which to choose.[24]
However, the practice differed fundamentally from
Schumpeter's formulation of the elitist position: "The
democratic method is that institutional arrangement
for arriving at political decisions in which individuals
acquire the power to decide by means of a competitive
struggle for the people's vote."[25] Schumpeter meant
power to decide quite literally: "The leaders of the
political parties decide, not 'the people.'"[26]

Not in Athens. Not even Pericles had such power.
While his influence was at its height, he could hope
for continual approval of his policies, expressed in the
people's vote in the Assembly, but his proposals were
submitted to the Assembly week in and week out, alternative views were before them, and the Assembly
always could, and on occasion did, abandon him and
his policies. The *decision* was theirs, not his or any

other leader's; recognition of the need for leadership was not accompanied by a surrender of the power of decision. And he knew it. It was not mere tactical politeness that led him to use the following words (as we are told) in 431 B.C. when he proposed rejection of a Spartan ultimatum and therefore a vote for war: "I see that on this occasion I must give you exactly the same advice as I have given in the past, and I call upon those of you who are persuaded to give your support to these resolutions which we are making all together" (Thucydides, 1.140.1).

In more conventional constitutional terms, the people possessed, not only eligibility for office-holding and the right to elect officials, but also the right to decide on all matters of public policy and the right to judge, sitting as a court, on all important cases, civil and criminal, public and private. The concentration of authority in the Assembly, the fragmentation and rotation of administrative posts, selection by lot, the absence of a paid bureaucracy, the popular jury-courts, all served to prevent the creation of a party machinery and therefore of an institutionalized political elite. Leadership was direct and personal; there was no place for mediocre puppets manipulated by the "real" leaders behind the scene.[27] Men like Pericles constituted a political elite, to be sure, but that elite was not self-perpetuating; membership in it was attained by public performance, primarily in the Assembly, access was open, and continued membership required continued performance.

Some of the institutional devices the Athenians were so imaginative in inventing lose their apparent oddity in the light of this political reality. Ostracism is the best known, a device whereby a man whose influence was judged to be dangerously excessive could be exiled up to ten years, though, significantly, without loss of property or civil status. The historical root of ostracism lay in tyranny and the fear of its recurrence, but the practice owes its survival to the almost intolerable insecurity of political leaders, who were driven, by the logic of the system, to try to protect themselves by removing from the scene physically the chief advocates of an alternative policy. In the absence of periodic elections among parties, what other way was there? And it is revealing that, when late in the fifth century B.C. ostracism degenerated into a nonfunctional device, the practice was quietly abandoned.

Another, even more curious, device was the one known as the *graphe paranomon,* whereby a man could be indicted and tried for making an "illegal proposal" in the Assembly.[28] It is impossible to fit this procedure into any conventional constitutional category. The Assembly's sovereignty was unlimited: for one brief moment late in the Peloponnesian War the Assembly was even manoeuvred into voting the abolition of democracy. Yet anyone who exercised his basic right of *ise-*

goria ran the risk of a severe penalty for a proposal he had the right to make, *even if that proposal had been passed by the Assembly.*

We cannot date the introduction of the *graphe paranomon* more exactly than some time in the fifth century B.C., and so we do not know the events that provoked it. Its function, however, is clear enough, a double one, of tempering *isegoria* with discipline and of giving the people, the *demos,* the opportunity to reconsider a decision they had themselves taken. A successful prosecution in a *graphe paranomon* had the effect of annulling a favourable Assembly vote, by the verdict not of an elite group such as the American Supreme Court but of the *demos* through the agency of a large popular jury-court selected by lot. Our system protects the freedom of representatives by parliamentary privilege, which paradoxically also protects their irresponsibility. The Athenian paradox was in the opposite direction, protecting the freedom of both the Assembly as a whole and its individual members by denying them immunity.

I have gone into detail about some of the mechanics of Athenian democracy not from antiquarian curiosity but in order to suggest that, despite the great divide from contemporary democracy, the ancient experience may not be so wholly irrelevant as modern political scientists think, specifically with respect to the controversial issue of leaders and followers. Mechanics and devices do not, of course, provide a sufficient expla-

nation; they can misfire as well as fulfil the function
for which they were designed. The Greeks themselves
did not develop a theory of democracy. There were
notions, maxims, generalities, but these do not add
up to a systematic theory. The philosophers attacked
democracy; the committed democrats responded by
ignoring them, by going about the business of government and politics in a democratic way, without writing
treatises on the subject.

One exception, possibly the only one, was the late
fifth-century B.C. Sophist, Protagoras, whose ideas are
known to us from the attack by Plato in one of his
earlier dialogues, the *Protagoras,* in which Socrates
mocks, parodies and even cheats to a degree that is
rare in the Platonic corpus.[29] Was this tone chosen by
Plato, one wonders, precisely because Protagoras not
only held characteristically Sophistical moral doctrines
but also developed a democratic political theory? The
essence of that theory, insofar as we can judge from
Plato, is that all men possess *politike techne,* the art of
political judgment, without which there can be no
civilized society. All men, at least all free men, are
peers in this respect, though not necessarily equal in
their skill in *politike techne*—a conception reminiscent
of the Declaration of Independence—and the conclusion follows that the Athenians were right to extend
isegoria to every citizen.

Politike techne did not alone define the human condition. Unlike the animal world, which lives by competition and aggression, men are by nature co-operative, possessing the qualities of *philia* (conventionally but pallidly translated as "friendship") and *dike*, justice. However, for Protagoras, friendship and justice would be insufficient for the genuine political community, the state, without the additional political sense. Significantly, Aristotle, who was no democrat, laid equal stress on friendship and justice as the two elements of *koinonia*, community. *Koinonia* is hard to translate by a single English word: it has a cluster of meanings, including, for example, business partnership, but here we must think of "community" with a strong inflection, as in the early Christian community, in which the bonds were not merely propinquity and a common way of life but also a consciousness of common destiny, common faith. For Aristotle man was by nature not only a being destined to live in a city-state but also a household being and a community being.

It was that sense of community, I suggest, fortified by the state religion, by their myths and their traditions, which was an essential element in the pragmatic success of the Athenian democracy (and which explains my rather long digression). Neither the sovereign Assembly, with its unlimited right of participation, nor the popular jury-courts nor the selection of officials by lot nor ostracism could have prevented either chaos on the one hand or tyranny on the other, had there not been the self-control among enough of the citizen-body to contain its own behaviour within bounds.

Self-control is very different from apathy, which means literally "lack of feeling," "insensibility," impermissible qualities in a genuine community. There was a tradition (Aristotle, *Constitution of Athens*, 8.5) that in his legislation early in the sixth century B.C. Solon passed the following law, specifically aimed against apathy: "When there is civil war in the city, anyone who does not take up arms on one side or the other shall be deprived of civil rights and of all share in the affairs of government." The authenticity of the law is doubtful, but not the sentiment. Pericles expressed it, in the same Funeral Oration in which he noted that poverty is no bar, by saying (Thucydides, 2.40.2): "A man may at the same time look after his own affairs and those of the state. . . . We consider anyone who does not share in the life of the citizen not as minding his own business but as useless."

It is to be noticed that Protagoras and Plato, poles apart though they were, each in his own way stressed the importance of education. I use the word not in its common contemporary sense of formal schooling but in an old-fashioned sense, in the ancient Greek sense: by *paideia* they meant upbringing, "formation" (German *Bildung*), the development of the moral virtues, of the sense of civic responsibility, of mature identification with the community, its traditions and values. In a small, homogeneous, relatively closed face-to-face society, it was perfectly valid to call the basic institutions of the community—the family, the dining-club, the gymnasium, the Assembly—agencies for education. A young man was educated by attending the Assembly; he learned, not necessarily the size of the island of Sicily (a purely technical question, as both Protagoras and Socrates would have agreed), but the political issues facing Athens, the choices, the arguments, and he learned to assess the men who put themselves forward as policy-makers, as leaders.

But what about larger, more complex societies? John Stuart Mill a century ago still thought Athens had something to offer. In his *Considerations on Representative Government,* he wrote as follows:

It is not sufficiently considered how little there is in most men's ordinary life to give any largeness either to their conceptions or to their sentiments . . . in most cases the individual has no access to any person of cultivation much superior to his own. Giving him something to do for the public, supplies, in a measure, all these deficiencies. If circumstances allow the amount of public duty assigned to him to be considerable, it makes him an educated man. Notwithstanding the defects of the social system and moral ideas of antiquity, the practice of the dicastery and the ecclesia [Assembly] raised the intellectual standard of an average Athenian citizen far beyond anything of which there is yet an example in any other mass of men, ancient or modern. . . . He is called upon, while so engaged, to weigh interests not his own; to be guided, in case of con-

flicting claims, by another rule than his private partialities;
to apply, at every turn, principles and maxims which have
for their reason of existence the common good: and he
usually finds associated with him in the same work minds
more familiarized than his own with these ideas and operations, whose study it will be to supply reasons to his understanding, and stimulation to his feeling for the general
interest.[30]

Mill's use of the present tense, in an essay published
in 1861, was no mere stylistic mannerism. "Almost all
travellers," he went on to comment, "are struck by the
fact that every American is in some sense both a patriot,
and a person of cultivated intelligence; and M. de
Tocqueville has shown how close the connection is between these qualities and their democratic institutions,"
how "wide" is the "diffusion of the ideas, tastes, and
sentiments of educated minds." [31] Mill, furthermore, was
no isolated theorist. He stood in the mainstream of
classical democratic theory, which was "informed by an
exceedingly ambitious purpose, the education of an entire people to the point where their intellectual, emotional, and moral capacities have reached their full
potential and they are joined, freely and actively, in a
genuine community. Beyond this magnificent general
purpose, classical democratic theory also embodies one
great strategy for the pursuit of this goal, the use of
political activity and government for the purposes of
public education. Governance is to be a continued effort
in mass education." [32]

Athens therefore provides a valuable case-study of how political leadership and popular participation succeeded in coexisting, over a long period of time, without either the apathy and ignorance exposed by public opinion experts, or the extremist nightmares that haunt elitist theorists. The Athenians made mistakes. Which governmental system has not? The familiar game of condemning Athens for not having lived up to some ideal of perfection is a stultifying approach. They made no fatal mistakes, and that is good enough. The failure of the Sicilian expedition in 415–413 B.C. was a technical command failure in the field, not the consequence of either ignorance or inadequate planning at home. Any autocrat or any "expert" politician could have made the same errors. Elitist theorists would be ill advised to count it as evidence on their side. If it is the case that Mill and classical democratic theory have now been falsified, that is not because they read history wrongly.*

Profound institutional changes have occurred since de Tocqueville and Mill wrote a century and more ago. The first is the radical transformation of the economy, dominated by supernational conglomerates to an extent not even imaginable to our forefathers. The new technology

---

* That Mill read the future wrongly is another matter. "The ever-increasing intervention of the people," he wrote approvingly in his review of de Tocqueville, "and of all classes of the people, in their own affairs, he regards as a cardinal maxim in the modern art of government" (*Dissertations and Discussions*, II, 8).

with which the economy works has placed an equally unprecedented power in the hands of whoever holds it, unprecedented in both its magnitude and its sophistication. In that category I include the mass media, both for their power to create and reinforce values and for the intellectual passivity they generate, which seems to me to be a denial of the "educational" goal of classical democratic theory.

Then there are significant new factors in the political field itself, above all, the conversion of politics into an occupation, in the narrow sense of that word and on a very large scale.[33] There have, of course, been other societies in which politicians or courtiers devoted themselves more or less fully to government—the late Roman Republic and the Roman Empire or modern autocracies—but these were not politicians in the strict sense, and certainly not in the democratic sense, and anyway their numbers were always small, their interests either individual or as representatives of an aristocratic estate, not those of an occupational group. One contemporary consequence is the close link between political occupation and money-making, with or without corruption, but I consider that a minor consequence compared with the creation of a new and powerful interest-group in society, the politicians.

"The reputation, indeed the political survival, of most leaders," wrote Henry Kissinger, "depends on their ability to realize their goals, however these may have been arrived at. Whether these goals are desirable is relatively less crucial." Leaders "reveal an almost compulsive desire to avoid even a temporary setback." Long-range interests are bound to be neglected "because the future has no administrative constituency." [34] This new interest-group, furthermore, is drawn from a narrow sector of the population; in the United States, so exclusively from lawyers and businessmen [35] that we find it hard to grasp the fact that as late as the end of the nineteenth century, a proportion of not only white-collar but even blue-collar workers participated actively in party leadership and public office, at least on the municipal level.[36] In Britain the same situation prevails, with a somewhat larger element of inherited wealth and commercial agriculture on the one side, and of teachers, journalists and union officials (a few of them manual workers in their youth) on the other.[37]

Finally, there is the staggering growth of the bureaucracy (in private institutions as in government). They are the experts, without whom modern society cannot possibly function, but the point has now been reached, in the size and hierarchical ramification of the bureaucracy, "where the stability of the internal 'political' system is preferred to the achievement of the functional goals of the organization." [38] In Mr. Kissinger's words, "What starts out as an aid to decision-makers often turns into a practically autonomous organization whose internal problems structure and sometimes compound the issues which it was originally designed to solve. . . . Sophistication may thus encourage paralysis or a crude popularization which defeats its own purpose." [39]

Under such conditions, it would be absurd to make any direct comparison with a small, homogeneous, face-to-face society such as ancient Athens; absurd to suggest, even to dream, that we might reinstate an Assembly of the citizens as the paramount decision-making body in a modern city or nation.* That is not the choice I have been considering, but an altogether different one, arising from political apathy and its evaluation. Public apathy and political ignorance are a fundamental fact today, beyond any possible dispute; decisions are made by political leaders, not by popular vote, which at best has only an occasional veto power after the fact. The issue is whether this state of affairs is, under modern conditions, a necessary and desirable one, or whether new forms of popular participation, in the Athenian spirit though not in the Athenian substance, if I may phrase it that way, need to be invented (I use the verb in the same sense in which I said earlier that the Athenians invented democracy). [40]

The elitist theory, with its "vision of the 'professional'

---

* Mill (*Dissertations and Discussions*, II, 19) slid into a false analogy when he wrote, "The newspapers and the railroads are solving the problem of bringing the democracy of England to vote, like that of Athens, simultaneously in one *agora*."

politician as hero," [41] with its call for "the end of ideology," with its conversion of an operational definition into a value-judgment, answers that question with a firm negative. "Democracy is not only or even primarily a means through which different groups can attain their ends or seek the good society: *it is the good society itself in operation*" (my italics).[42] Such a judgment, it has been well said by a recent critic, is "a codification of past accomplishments . . . it vindicates the main features of the status quo and provides a model for tidying up loose ends. Democracy becomes a system to be preserved not an end to be sought. Those who wish a guide to the future must look elsewhere." [43] That seems to me to be a correct *historical* judgment. Whether or not it is also a correct *political* judgment every man will decide for himself.

2 Athenian Demagogues

When the news of their defeat in Sicily in 413 B.C. reached the Athenians, they received it with disbelief. Then came the realization of the full scale of the disaster, and the people, writes Thucydides (8.1.1), "were indignant with the orators who had joined in promoting the expedition, as if they [the people] had not themselves decreed it [in assembly]." To this George Grote made the following rejoinder: "From these latter words, it would seem that Thucydides considered the Athenians, after having adopted the expedition by their votes, to have debarred themselves from the right of complaining of those speakers who had stood forward prominently to advise the step. I do not at all concur in his opinion. The adviser of any important measure always makes himself morally responsible for its justice, usefulness, and practicability, and he very properly incurs disgrace, more or less according to the case, if it turns out

Originally published in *Past and Present* 21 (1962): 3–24, and reprinted in somewhat revised form. © The Past and Present Society; reprinted by their kind permission.

to present results totally contrary to those which he had predicted."[1]

These two opposing quotations raise all the fundamental problems inherent in the Athenian democracy: the problems of policy-making and leadership, of decisions and the responsibility for them. Unfortunately Thucydides (6.1–25) tells us very little about the orators who successfully urged on the Assembly the decision to mount the great invasion of Sicily. In fact, he tells us nothing concrete about the meeting, other than that the people were given misinformation by a delegation from the Sicilian city of Segesta and by their own envoys just returned from Sicily, and that most of those who voted were so ignorant of the relevant facts that they did not even know the size of the island or of its population.

Five days later a second Assembly was held to authorize the necessary armament. The general Nicias took the opportunity to seek a reversal of the whole programme. He was opposed by a number of speakers, Athenian and Sicilian, who are neither named by the historian nor described in any way, and by Alcibiades, who is given a speech which throws much light on Thucydides himself and on his judgment of Alcibiades, but scarcely any on the issues, neither the immediate ones being debated nor the broader ones of democratic procedure and leadership. The result was a complete defeat for Nicias. Everyone, Thucydides admits, was then more eager than before to go ahead with the plan—the old and the young, the hoplite soldiers (who were drawn from the wealthier half of the citizenry) and the common people alike. The few who remained opposed, he concludes, refrained from voting lest they appear unpatriotic.

The wisdom of the Sicilian expedition is a very difficult matter. Thucydides himself had more than one view at different times in his life. However, he seems not to have changed his mind about the orators: they promoted the expedition for the wrong reasons and they gained the day by playing on the ignorance and emotions of the Assembly. Alcibiades, he says, pressed hardest of all, because he wished to thwart Nicias, because he was personally ambitious and hoped to gain fame and wealth from his generalship in the campaign, and because his extravagant and licentious tastes were more expensive than he could really afford. Elsewhere, writing in more general terms, Thucydides says this (2.65.9–11): under Pericles "the government was a democracy in name but in reality ruled by the first citizen. His successors were more equal to each other, and each seeking to become the first man they even offered the conduct of affairs to the whims of the people. This, as was to be expected in a great state ruling an empire, produced many blunders."

In short, after the death of Pericles Athens fell into

the hands of demagogues and was ruined. Thucydides does not use the word "demagogue" in any of the passages I have been discussing. It is an uncommon word with him[2] as it is in Greek literature generally, and that fact may come as a surprise, for there is no more familiar theme in the Athenian picture (despite the rarity of the word) than the demagogue and his adjutant, the sycophant. The demagogue is a bad thing: to "lead the people" is to mislead—above all, to mislead by failing to lead. The demagogue is driven by self-interest, by the desire to advance himself in power, and through power, in wealth. To achieve this, he surrenders all principles, all genuine leadership, and he panders to the people in every way—in Thucydides' words, "even offering the conduct of affairs to the whims of the people." This picture is drawn not only directly, but also in reverse. Here, for example, is Thucydides' image of the right kind of leader (2.65.8): "Because of his prestige, intelligence and known incorruptibility with respect to money, Pericles was able to lead the people as a free man should. He led them instead of being led by them. He did not have to humour them in the pursuit of power; on the contrary, his repute was such that he could contradict them and provoke their anger."

This was not everyone's judgment. Aristotle puts the breakdown earlier: it was after Ephialtes took

away the power of the Council of the Areopagus that
the passion for demagogy set in. Pericles, he contin-
ues, first acquired political influence by prosecuting
Cimon for malfeasance in office; he energetically pursued a policy of naval power, "which gave the lower
classes the audacity to take over the leadership in
politics more and more"; and he introduced pay for
jury service, thus bribing the people with their own
money. These were demagogic practices and they
brought Pericles to power, which, Aristotle agrees,
he then used well and properly.[3]

But my interest is neither in evaluating Pericles
as an individual nor in examining the lexicography of
demagogy. The Greek political vocabulary was normally vague and imprecise, apart from formal titles
for individual offices or bodies (and often enough not
even then). All writers accepted the need for political
leadership as axiomatic; their problem was to distin-
guish between good and bad types. With respect to
Athens and its democracy, the word "demagogue" understandably became the simplest way of identify-
ing the bad type, and it does not matter in the least
whether the word appears in any given text or not.
I suppose it was Aristophanes who established the
model in his portrayal of Cleon, yet he never directly
applied the noun "demagogue" to him or anyone
else.[4] Similarly, Thucydides surely thought that Cleophon, Hyperbolus, and some, if not all, of the orators

responsible for the Sicilian disaster were demagogues, but he never attached the word to any of these men.

It is important to stress the word "type," for the issue raised by Greek writers is one of the essential *qualities* of the leader, not (except very secondarily) his techniques or technical competence, nor even (except in a very generalized way) his programme and policies. The crucial distinction is between the man who gives leadership with nothing else in mind but the good of the state, and the man whose self-interest makes his own position paramount and urges him to pander to the people. The former may make a mistake and adopt the wrong policy in any given situation; the latter may at times make sound proposals, as when Alcibiades dissuaded the fleet at Samos from jeopardizing the naval position by rushing back to Athens in 411 B.C. to overthrow the oligarchs who had seized power there, an action to which Thucydides (8.86) gave explicit approval. But these are not fundamental distinctions. Nor are other traits attributed to individual demagogues: Cleon's habit of shouting when addressing the Assembly, personal dishonesty in money matters, and so on. Such things merely sharpen the picture. From Aristophanes to Aristotle, the attack on the demagogues always falls back on the one central question: in whose interest does the leader lead?

Behind this formulation of the question lay three

propositions. The first is that men are unequal, both in their moral worth and capability and in their social and economic status. The second is that any community tends to divide into factions, the most fundamental of which are the rich and well-born on one side, the poor on the other, each with its own qualities, potentialities, and interests. The third proposition is that the well-ordered and well-run state is one which overrides faction and serves as an instrument for the good life.

Faction is the greatest evil and the most common danger. "Faction" is a conventional English translation of the Greek *stasis,* one of the most remarkable words to be found in any language. Its root-sense is "placing," "setting" or "stature," "station." Its range of political meanings can best be illustrated by merely stringing out the definitions to be found in the lexicon: "party," "party formed for seditious purposes," "faction," "sedition," "discord," "division," "dissent," and, finally, a well-attested meaning which the lexicon incomprehensibly omits, namely, "civil war" or "revolution." Unlike "demagogue," *stasis* is a very common word in the literature, and its connotation is regularly pejorative. Oddly enough, it has been a relatively neglected concept in modern study of Greek history.[5] The implication has not been drawn often enough or sharply enough, I believe, that there must be deep significance in the fact that a word which has the original sense of "station" or "position," and which, in abstract logic, could have an equally neutral sense when used in a political context, in practice does nothing of the kind, but immediately takes on the nastiest overtones. A political position, a partisan position—that is the inescapable implication—is a bad thing, leading to sedition, civil war, and the disruption of the social fabric. And this same tendency is repeated throughout the language. There is no eternal law, after all, why "demagogue," a "leader of the people," must become "mis-leader of the people." Or why *hetairia*, an old Greek word which means, among other things, "club" or "society," should in fifth-century Athens have come simultaneously to mean "conspiracy" and "seditious organization." Whatever the explanation, it lies not in philology but in Greek society itself.

No one who has read the Greek political writers can have failed to notice the unanimity of approach in this respect. Whatever the disagreements among them, they all insist that the state must stand outside class or other factional interests. Its aims and objectives are moral, timeless, and universal, and they can be achieved—more correctly, approached or approximated—only by education, moral conduct (especially on the part of those in authority), morally correct legislation, and the choice of the right governors. The existence of classes and interests as an empirical fact is, of course, not denied. What is denied is that the choice of political goals can legitimately be linked with these classes and interests, or that the good of the state can be advanced except by ignoring (if not suppressing) private interests.

It was Plato who pursued this line of its reasoning to its most radical solutions. In the *Gorgias* (502E-519D) he had argued that not even the great Athenian political figures of the past—Miltiades, Themistocles, Cimon and Pericles—were true statesmen. They had merely been more accomplished than their successors in gratifying the desires of the *demos* with ships and walls and dockyards. They had failed to make the citizens better men, and to call them "statesmen" was therefore to confuse the pastrycook with the doctor. Then, in the *Republic*, Plato proposed to concentrate all power in the hands of a small, select, appropriately educated class, who were to be freed from all special interests by the most radical measures: denying them both private property and the family. Only under these conditions would they behave as perfect moral agents, leading the state to its proper goals without the possibility that any self-interest might intrude.

Plato, to be sure, was the most untypical of men. One cannot safely generalize from Plato to all Greeks, nor even to any other single Greek. Who else shared his passionate conviction that qualified experts—philosophers—could make (and should therefore be empowered to enforce) universally correct and authoritative decisions about the good life, the life of virtue, which was the sole end of the state?"[6] Yet regarding the one problem with which I am immediately concerned—private interests and the state—Plato stood on common ground with many Greek writers (much as they disagreed with him on the solutions). In the great final scene of Aeschylus' *Eumenides* the chorus expresses the doctrine explicitly: the welfare of the state can rest only on harmony and freedom from faction. Thucydides implies this more than once.[7] And it underlies the theory of the mixed constitution as we already find it in Aristotle's *Politics*.

The most empirical of Greek philosophers, Aristotle collected vast quantities of data about the actual workings of Greek states, including facts about *stasis*. The *Politics* includes an elaborate taxonomy of *stasis*, and even advice on how *stasis* can be avoided under a variety of conditions. But Aristotle's canons and goals were ethical, his work a branch of moral philosophy. He viewed political behaviour teleologically, according to the moral ends which are man's by his nature, and he believed that those ends are subverted if the governors make their decisions out of personal or class interest. That was the test by which he distinguished between the three "right" forms of government ("according to absolute justice") and their degenerate forms: monarchy becomes tyranny when an individual rules in his own interest rather than in the interest of the whole state, aristocracy similarly becomes oligarchy, and polity becomes democracy (or, in the language of Polybius, democracy becomes mobrule).[8] Among democracies, furthermore, those in rural communities will be superior because farmers are too occupied to bother with meetings, whereas urban craftsmen and shopkeepers find it easy to attend, and such people "are generally a bad lot."[9]

The great difference between political analysis and moral judgment could not be better exemplified than in the passage by the "Old Oligarch" I quoted in chapter 1: "As for the Athenian system of government, I do not like it. However, since they decided to become a democracy, it seems to me that they are preserving the democracy well."[10] Do not be misled, says the author in effect: I and some of you dislike democracy, but a reasoned consideration of the facts shows that what we condemn on moral grounds is very strong as a practical force, and its strength lies in its immorality. This is a very promising line of investigation, but it was not pursued in antiquity. Instead, those thinkers whose orientation was anti-democratic persisted in their concentration on political philosophy. And those who sided with the democracy? A.H.M. Jones tried to formulate the democratic theory from the fragmentary evidence available in the surviving literature, most of it from the fourth century.[11] Then Eric Havelock made a massive attempt to discover what he called the "liberal temper" in fifth-century Athenian politics, chiefly from the fragments of the pre-Socratic philosophers. In reviewing his book, Momigliano suggested that the effort was foredoomed because "it is not absolutely certain that a well-articulated democratic idea existed in the fifth-century."[12]

I have already indicated in the previous chapter that I do not believe that an articulated democratic theory ever existed in Athens. There were notions, maxims, generalities—which Jones has assembled —but they do not add up to a systematic theory. And why indeed should they? It is a curious fallacy to suppose that every social or governmental system in history must necessarily have been accompanied by an elaborate theoretical system. Where that does occur it is often the work of lawyers, and Athens had no jurists in the proper sense. Or it may be the work of philosophers, but the systematic philosophers of this period had a set of concepts and values incompatible with democracy. We must attempt on our own to make the analysis the Athenians failed to make for themselves.

No account of the Athenian democracy can have any validity if it overlooks four points, each obvious in itself. The first is that this was a direct democracy, and however much such a system may have in common with representative democracy, the two differ in certain fundamental respects, and particularly on the very issues with which I am here concerned. The second point is what Ehrenberg calls the "narrowness of space" of the Greek city-state, an appreciation of which, he has rightly stressed, is crucial to an understanding of its political life.[13] The implications were summed up by Aristotle in a famous passage: "A state composed of too many . . . will not be a true state, for the simple reason that it can hardly have a true constitution. Who can be the general of a mass so excessively large? And who can be herald, except Stentor?" (*Politics* 1326b3–7).

The third point is that the Assembly was the crown of the system, possessing the right and the power to make all the policy decisions, in actual practice with few limitations, either of precedent or of scope. (Strictly speaking there was appeal from the Assembly to the popular courts with their large lay membership. Nevertheless, I ignore the courts in much, though not all, of what follows, because I believe, as the Athenians did themselves, that although the courts complicated the practical mechanism of politics, they were an expression, not a reduction, of the absolute power of the people functioning directly, and because I believe that the operational analysis I am trying to make would not be significantly altered and would perhaps be obscured if in this brief compass I did not concentrate on the Assembly.) The Assembly, finally, was nothing other than an open-air mass meeting on the hill called the Pnyx, and the fourth point therefore is that we are dealing with problems of crowd behavior; the psychology and laws of behavior at work in the Assembly could not have been identical with those at work in the small group, or even in the larger kind of body of which a modern parliament is an example (though, it must be admitted, we can do little more today than acknowledge the existence of these influences).

Who were the Assembly? That is a question we cannot answer satisfactorily. Every male citizen automatically became eligible to attend when he reached his eighteenth birthday, and he retained that privilege to his death (except for the small number who lost their civic rights for one reason or another). In Pericles' time the number eligible was of the order of 35,000 or 40,000. Women were excluded; so were the fairly numerous non-citizens who were free men, nearly all of them Greeks, but outsiders in the political sphere; and so were the far more numerous slaves. All figures are a guess, but it would not be wildly inaccurate to suggest that the adult male citizens comprised about one sixth of the total population (taking town and countryside together). But the critical question to be determined is how many of the

40,000 actually went to meetings. It is reasonable to imagine that under normal conditions the attendance came chiefly from the urban residents. Fewer peasants would have taken the journey in order to attend a meeting of the Assembly.[14] Therefore one large section of the eligible population was, with respect to direct participation, excluded. That is something to know, but it does not get us far enough. We can guess for example, with the aid of a few hints in the sources, that the composition was normally weighted on the side of the more aged and the more well-to-do men—but that is only a guess, and the degree of weighting is beyond even guessing.

Still, one important fact can be fixed, namely, that each meeting of the Assembly was unique in its composition. There was no membership in the Assembly as such, only membership in a given Assembly on a given day. Perhaps the shifts were not significant from meeting to meeting in quiet, peaceful times when no vital issues were being debated. Yet even then an important element of predictability was lacking. When he entered the Assembly, no policy-maker could be quite sure that a change in the composition of the audience had not occurred, whether through accident or through more or less organised mobilization of some particular sector of the population, which could tip the balance of the votes against a decision made at a previous meeting. And times were often neither peaceful nor normal. In the final decade of the Peloponnesian War, to take an extreme example, the whole rural population was compelled to abandon the countryside and live within the city walls. It is beyond reasonable belief that during this period there was not a larger proportion of countrymen at meetings than was normal. A similar situation prevailed for briefer periods at other times, when an enemy army was operating in Attica. We need not interpret Aristophanes literally when he opens the *Acharnians* with a soliloquy by a farmer who is sitting in the Pnyx waiting for the Assembly to begin and saying to himself how he hates the city and everyone in it and how he intends to shout down any speaker who proposes anything except peace. But Cleon could not have afforded the luxury of ignoring this strange element seated on the hillside before him. They might upset a policy line which he had been able to carry while the Assembly had a majority of city-dwellers.

The one clearcut instance came in the year 411. Then the Assembly was terrorized into voting the democracy out of existence, and it was surely no accident that this occurred at a time when the fleet was fully mobilized and stationed on the island of Samos. The citizens who served in the navy were drawn from the poor and they were known to be the staunchest supporters of the democratic system in its late fifth-century form. Being in Samos, they could not be in Athens, thus enabling the oligarchs to win the day through a majority in the Assembly which was not only a minority of the eligible members but an untypical minority. Our sources do not permit us to study the history of Athenian policy systematically with such knowledge at our disposal, but surely the men who led Athens were acutely aware of the possibility of a change in the composition of the Assembly, and included it in their tactical calculations.

Each meeting, furthermore, was complete in itself. Granted that much preparatory work was done by the Council (*boule*), that informal canvassing took place, and that there were certain devices to control and check frivolous or irresponsible motions, it is nevertheless true that the normal procedure was for a proposal to be introduced, debated, and either passed (with or without amendment) or rejected in a single continuous sitting. We must reckon, therefore, not only with narrowness of space but also with narrowness of time, and with the pressures that generated, especially on leaders (and would-be leaders). I have already mentioned the case of the Sicilian expedition, which was decided in principle on one day and then planned, so to speak, five days later when the scale and cost were discussed and voted.

Another kind of case is that of the well-known Mytilene debate. Early in the Peloponnesian War the city of Mytilene revolted from the Athenian Empire. The rebellion was crushed and the Athenian Assembly decided to make an example of the Mytileneans by putting the entire male population to death. Revulsion of feeling set in at once, the issue was reopened at another meeting the very next day, and the decision was reversed (Thucydides 3.27–50). Cleon, at that time the most important political figure in Athens, advocated the policy of frightfulness. The second Assembly was a personal defeat for him—he had participated in the debates on both days—though he seems not to have lost his status even temporarily as a result (as he well might have). But how does one measure the psychological effect on him of such a twenty-four hour reversal? How does one estimate not only its impact, but also his awareness all through his career as a leader that such a possibility was a constant factor in Athenian politics? I cannot answer such questions concretely, but I submit that the weight could have been no light one. Cleon surely appreciated, as we cannot, what it promised for men like himself that in the second year of the Peloponnesian War, when morale was temporarily shattered by the plague, the people turned on Pericles, fined him heavily, and deposed him for a brief period from the office of general (Thucydides 2.65.1–4). If this could happen to Pericles, who was immune?

In the Mytilene case Thucydides' account suggests

that Cleon's was a lost cause the second day, that he tried to persuade the Assembly to abandon a course of action which they intended to pursue from the moment the session opened, and that he failed. But the story of the meeting in 411, as Thucydides (8.53–54) tells it, is a different one. Pisander began the day with popular feeling against his proposal that the introduction of an oligarchical form of government should be considered, and he ended it with a victory. The actual debate had swung enough votes to give him a majority.

Debate designed to win votes among an outdoor audience numbering many thousands means oratory, in the strict sense of the word. It was therefore perfectly precise language to call political leaders "orators," as a synonym and not merely, as we might do, as a mark of the particular skill of a particular political figure.[15] Under Athenian conditions, however, much more is implied. The picture of the Assembly I have been trying to draw suggests not only oratory, but also a "spontaneity" of debate and decision which parliamentary democracy lacks, at least in our day.[16] Everyone, speakers and audience alike, knew that before night fell the issue must be decided, that each man present would vote "freely" (without fear of whips or other party controls) and purposefully, and therefore that every speech, every argument must seek to persuade the audience on the spot, that it was all a serious performance, as a whole and in each of its parts.

I place the word "freely" within quotation marks for the last thing I wish to imply is the activity of a free, disembodied rational faculty, that favourite illusion of so much political theory since the Enlightenment. Members of the Assembly were free from the controls which bind the members of a parliament: they held no office, they were not elected, and therefore they could neither be punished nor rewarded in subsequent elections for their voting records. But they were not free from the human condition, from habit and tradition, from the influences of family and friends, of class and status, of personal experiences, resentments, prejudices, values, aspirations, and fears, much of it in the subconscious. These they took with them when they went up on the Pnyx, and with these they listened to the debates and made up their minds, under conditions very different from the voting practices of our day. There is a vast difference between voting on infrequent occasions for a man or a party on the one hand, and on the other hand voting every few days directly on the issues themselves. In Aristotle's time the Assembly met at least four times in each thirty-six day period. Whether this was also the rule in the fifth century is not known,

but there were occasions, as during the Peloponnesian War, when meetings took place even
more frequently.

Then there were the two other factors I have
already mentioned, the smallness of the Athenian
world, in which every member of the Assembly knew
personally many others sitting on the Pnyx, and the
mass-meeting background of the voting—a situation
virtually unrelated to the impersonal act of marking a
voting paper in physical isolation from every other
voter, an act we perform, furthermore, with the
knowledge that millions of other men and women are
simultaneously doing the same thing in many places,
some of them hundreds of miles distant. When, for
example, Alcibiades and Nicias rose in the Assembly
in 415, the one to propose the expedition against Sicily, the other to argue against it, each knew that,
should the motion be carried, one or both would be
asked to command in the field. And in the audience
there were many who were being asked to vote on
whether they, personally, would march out in a few
days, as officers, soldiers, or members of the fleet.
Such examples can be duplicated in a number of
other, scarcely less vital areas: taxation, food supply,
pay for jury duty, extension of the franchise, laws of
citizenship, and so on.

To be sure, much of the activity of the Assembly
was in a lower key, largely occupied with technical

measures (such as cult regulations) or ceremonial acts (such as honorary decrees for a great variety of individuals). It would be a mistake to imagine Athens as a city in which week in and week out great issues dividing the population were being debated and decided. But on the other hand, there were very few single years (and certainly no ten-year periods) in which some great issue did not arise: the two Persian invasions, the long series of measures which completed the process of democratization, the empire, the Peloponnesian War (which occupied twenty-seven years) and its two oligarchic interludes, the endless diplomatic manoeuvres and wars of the fourth century, with their attendant fiscal crises, all culminating in the decades of Philip and Alexander. It did not often happen, as it did to Cleon in the dispute over Mytilene, that a politician was faced with a repeat performance the following day; but the Assembly did meet constantly, without long periods of holiday or recess. The week-by-week conduct of a war, for example, had to go before the Assembly week by week, as if Winston Churchill were to have been compelled to take a referendum before each move in World War II, and then to face another vote after the move was made, in the Assembly or the law-courts, to determine not merely what the next step should be but also whether he was to be dismissed and his plans abandoned, or even whether he was to be held criminally culpable, subject to a fine or exile, or, conceivably, given the death penalty either for the proposal itself or for the way the previous move had been carried out. It was part of the Athenian governmental system that, in addition to the endless challenge in the Assembly, a politician was faced, equally without respite, with the threat of politically inspired lawsuits.

If I insist on the psychological aspect, it is not to ignore the considerable political experience of many men who voted in the Assembly—experience gained in the Council, the law-courts, the demes, and the Assembly itself—nor is it merely to counter what I have called the disembodied-rationalism conception. I want to stress something very positive, namely, the intense degree of involvement which attendance at the Athenian Assembly entailed. And this intensity was equally (or even more strongly) the case among the orators, for each vote judged them as well as the issue to be decided on. If I had to choose one word which best characterized the condition of being a political leader in Athens, the word would be "tension."

In some measure that is true of all politicians who are subject to a vote. "The desperateness of politics and government" is R. B. McCallum's telling phrase, which he then developed in this way: "Certainly a note of cynicism and weariness with the manoeuvres and posturings of party politicians is natural and to an extent proper to discerning dons and civil ser-

vants, who can reflect independently and at leisure
on the doings of their harried masters in government.
But this seems to arise from a deliberate rejection
. . . of the aims and ideals of party statesmen and
their followers and the continual responsibility for the
security and well-being in the state. For one thing
party leaders are in some sense apostles, although all
may not be Gladstones; there are policies to which
they dedicate themselves and policies which alarm
and terrify them." [17]

I believe this to be a fair description of Athenian
leaders, too, despite the absence of political parties,
equally applicable to Themistocles as to Aristides, to
Pericles as to Cimon, to Cleon as to Nicias; for, it
should be obvious, this kind of judgment is independent of any judgment about the merits or weaknesses
of a particular programme or policy. More accurately,
I should have said that this understates the case for
the Athenians. Their leaders had *no* respite. Because
their influence had to be earned and exerted directly
and immediately—this was a necessary consequence
of a direct, as distinct from a representative, democracy—they had to lead in person, and they had also
to bear, in person, the brunt of the opposition's at-
tacks. More than that, they walked alone. They had
their lieutenants, of course, and politicians made alli-
ances with each other. But these were fundamentally
personal links, shifting frequently, useful in helping

to carry through a particular measure or even a group of measures, but lacking that quality of support, that buttressing or cushioning effect, which is provided by a bureaucracy or a political party, in another way by an institutionalized establishment like the Roman Senate. The critical point is that there was no "government" in the modern sense. There were posts and offices, but none had any standing in the Assembly. A man was a leader solely as a function of his personal, and in the literal sense, unofficial status within the Assembly itself. The test of whether or not he held that status was simply whether the Assembly did or did not vote as he wished, and therefore the test was repeated with each proposal.

These were the conditions which faced all leaders in Athens, not merely those whom Thucydides and Plato dismissed as "demagogues," not merely those whom some modern historians mis-call "radical democrats," but everyone, aristocrat or commoner, altruist or self-seeker, able or incompetent, who, in George Grote's phrase, "stood forward prominently to advise" the Athenians. No doubt the motives which moved men to stand forward varied greatly. But that does not matter in this context, for each one of them without exception, *chose* to aspire to, and actively to work and contest for, leadership, knowing just what that entailed, including the risks. Within narrow limits, they all had to use the same techniques, too.

Cleon's platform manner may have been inelegant and boisterous, but how serious is Aristotle's remark (*Constitution of Athens* 28.3) that he was the first man to "shout and rail"? Are we to imagine that Thucydides the son of Melesias (and kinsman of the historian) and Nicias whispered when they addressed the Assembly in opposition to Pericles and Cleon, respectively? Or that Thucydides brought his upperclass backers into the Assembly and seated them together to form a claque?[18]

This is obviously a frivolous approach. As Aristotle noted (*Constitution of Athens* 28.1), the death of Pericles marked a turning-point in the social history of Athenian leadership. Until then they seem to have been drawn from the old aristocratic landed families, including the men who were responsible for carrying out the reforms which completed the democracy. After Pericles a new class of leaders emerged. Despite the familiar prejudicial references to Cleon the tanner or Cleophon the lyre-maker, these were in fact not poor men, not craftsmen and labourers turned politician, but men of means who differed from their predecessors in their ancestry and their outlook, and who provoked resentment and hostility for their presumption in breaking the old monopoly of leadership.[19] When such attitudes are under discussion, one can always turn to Xenophon to find the lowest level of explanation (which is not therefore necessarily the wrong one). One of the most important of the new leaders was a man called Anytus, who, like Cleon before him, drew his wealth from a slave tannery. Anytus had a long and distinguished career, but he was also the chief actor in the prosecution of Socrates. What is Xenophon's explanation? Simply that Socrates had publicly berated Anytus for bringing up his son to follow in his trade instead of educating him as a proper gentleman, and that Anytus, in revenge for this personal insult, had Socrates tried and executed (*Apology* 30–32).

None of this is to deny that there were very fundamental issues behind the thick façade of prejudice and abuse. Throughout the fifth century there were the twin issues of democracy (or oligarchy) and empire, brought to a climax in the Peloponnesian War. Defeat in the war ended the empire and it soon also ended the debate about the kind of government Athens was to have. Oligarchy ceased to be a serious issue in practical politics. Only the persistence of the philosophers creates an illusion about it; they continued to argue fifth-century issues in the fourth century, but politically in a vacuum. Down to the middle of the fourth century, the actual policy questions were perhaps less dramatic than before, though not necessarily less vital to the participants: such matters as navy, finance, foreign relations both with Persia and with other Greek states, and the ever-present problem of corn supply. Then came the final great conflict, over the rising power of Macedon. That debate went on for some three decades, and it ended only in the year following the death of Alexander the Great when the Macedonian army put an end to democracy itself in Athens.

All these were questions about which men could legitimately disagree, and with passion. On the issues, the arguments of, for example, Plato require earnest consideration, but only in so far as he addressed himself to the issues. The injection of the charge of demagogy into the polemic amounts to a resort to the very same unacceptable debating tricks for which the so-called demagogues are condemned. Suppose, for example, that Thucydides was right in attributing Alcibiades' advocacy of the Sicilian expedition to his personal extravagance and to various discreditable private motives. What relevance has that to the merits of the proposal itself? Would the Sicilian expedition, as a war measure, have been a better idea if Alcibiades had been an angelic youth? To ask the question is to dismiss it, and all other such arguments with it. One must dismiss as summarily the objections to oratory: by definition, to wish to lead Athens implies the burden of trying to persuade Athens, and an essential part of that effort consisted in public oratory.

One can draw distinctions, of course. I should concede the label "demagogue" in its most pejorative sense, for example, if a campaign were built around promises which a clique of orators neither intended to honour nor were capable of honouring. But, significantly enough, this accusation is rarely levelled against the so-called demagogues, and the one definite instance we know of comes from the other camp. The oligarchy of 411 was sold to the Athenians on the appeal that this was now the only way to obtain Persian support and thus to win the otherwise lost war. Even on the most favourable view, as Thucydides makes quite clear (8.68–91), Pisander and some of his associates may have meant this originally but they quickly abandoned all pretence of trying to win the war while they concentrated on preserving the newly won oligarchy on as narrow a base as possible. That is what I should call "demagogy," if the word is to merit its pejorative flavour. That is "misleading the people" in the literal sense.

But what then of the interest question, of the supposed clash between the interests of the whole state and the interests of a section or faction within the state? Is that not a valid distinction? It is a pity that we have no direct evidence (and no indirect evidence of any value) about the way the long debate was conducted between 508 B.C., when Clisthenes established the democracy in its primitive form, and the later years of Pericles' dominance. Those were the

years when class interests would most likely have
been expounded openly and bluntly. Actual speeches
survive only from the end of the fifth century on, and
they reveal what anyone could have guessed who had
not been blinded by Plato and others, namely, that
the appeal was customarily a national one, not a factional one. There is little open pandering to the poor
against the rich, to the farmers against the town or to
the town against the farmers. Why indeed should
there have been?

At the same time a politician cannot ignore class
or sectional interests or the conflicts among them,
whether in a constituency today or in the Assembly
in ancient Athens. The evidence for Athens suggests
that on many issues—the empire and the Peloponnesian War, for example, or relations with Philip of
Macedon—the divisions over policy did not closely
follow class or sectional lines. But other questions,
such as that of opening the archonship and other
offices to men of the lower property censuses or that
of pay for jury service, or, in the fourth century, the
financing of the fleet or the theoric fund, were by
their nature class issues. Advocates on both sides
knew this and knew how and when (and when not) to
make their appeals accordingly, at the same time that
they each argued, and believed, that only their
respective points of view would advance Athens as a
whole. To plead against Ephialtes and Pericles that

eunomia, the well-ordered state ruled by law, had the higher moral claim, was merely a plea for the status quo dressed up in fancy language.[20]

In his little book on the Athenian constitution, Aristotle wrote the following (27.3–4): "Pericles was the first to give pay for jury service, as a demagogic measure to counter the wealth of Cimon. The latter, who possessed the fortune of a tyrant . . . supported many of his fellow-demesmen, every one of whom was free to come daily and receive from him enough for his sustenance. Besides, none of his estates was enclosed, so that anyone who wished could take from its fruits. Pericles' property did not permit such largesse, and on the advice of Damonides . . . he distributed among the people from what was their own . . . and so he introduced pay for the jurors."

Aristotle himself, as I indicated earlier, praised Pericles' regime and he refused responsibility for this explanation, but others who repeated it, both before and after him, thought it was a telling instance of demagogy pandering to the common people. The obvious retort is to ask whether what Cimon did was not pandering in equal measure, or whether opposition to pay for jury service was not pandering, too, but in that case to the men of property. No useful analysis is possible in such terms, for they serve only to conceal the real grounds for disagreement. If one is opposed to full democracy as a form of govern-

ment, then it is wrong to encourage popular participation in the juries by offering pay; but it is wrong
because the objective is wrong, not because Pericles
obtained leadership status by proposing and carrying
the measure. And vice versa, if one favours a democratic system.

What emerges from all this is a very simple proposition, namely, that demagogues—I use the word in a
neutral sense—were a structural element in the Athenian political system. By this I mean, first, that the
system could not function at all without them; secondly, that the term is equally applicable to all leaders, regardless of class or point of view; and thirdly,
that within rather broad limits they are to be judged
individually not by their manners or their methods,
but by their performance. (And that, I need hardly
add, is precisely how they *were* judged in life, if not
in books.) Up to a point one can easily parallel the
Athenian demagogue with the modern politician, but
there soon comes a point when distinctions must be
drawn, not merely because the work of government
has become so much more complex, but more basically because of the differences between a direct and
a representative democracy. I have already discussed
the mass-meeting (with its uncertain composition),
the lack of a bureaucracy and a party system, and the
resulting state of continuous tension in which an Athenian demagogue lived and worked. But there is one

consequence which needs a little examination, for these conditions make up an important part (if not the whole) of the explanation of an apparently negative feature of Athenian politics, and of Greek politics generally. David Hume put it this way: "To exclude faction from a free government, is very difficult, if not altogether impracticable; but such inveterate rage between the factions, and such bloody maxims are found, in modern times, amongst religious parties alone. In ancient history we may always observe, where one party prevailed, whether the nobles or people (for I can observe no difference in this respect), that they immediately butchered . . . and banished . . . No form of process, no law, no trial, no pardon. . . . These people were extremely fond of liberty, but seem not to have understood it very well. [21]

The remarkable thing about Athens is how near she came to being the complete exception to this correct observation of Hume's, to being free, in other words, from *stasis* in its ultimate meaning. The democracy was established in 508 B.C. following a brief civil war. Thereafter, in its history of nearly two centuries, armed terror, butchery without process or law, was employed on only two occasions, in 411 and 404, both times by oligarchic factions which seized control of the state for brief periods. And the second time, in particular, the democratic faction, when it regained power, was generous and law-abiding in its treatment of the oligarchs, so much so that praise has been attributed even from Plato. Writing about the restoration of 403, he is supposed to have said that "no one should be surprised that some men took savage personal revenge against their enemies in this revolution, but in general the returning party behaved equitably."[22] This is not to suggest that the two centuries were totally free from individual acts of injustice and brutality. Hume—speaking of Greece generally and not of Athens in particular—observed "no difference in this respect" between the factions. We seem to have a less clear vision of Athens, reflected in the distorting mirror of men like Thucydides, Xenophon and Plato, which magnifies the exceptional incidents of extreme democratic intolerance—such as the trial and execution of the generals who won the battle of Arginusae and the trial and execution of Socrates—while it minimizes and often obliterates altogether the behaviour on the other side, for example, the political assassination of Ephialtes in 462 or 461 and of Androcles in 411, each in his time the most influential of the popular leaders.

If Athens largely escaped the extreme forms of *stasis* so common elsewhere, she could not escape its lesser manifestations. Athenian politics had an all-or-nothing quality. The objective on each side was not merely to defeat the opposition but to crush it, to be-

head it by destroying its leaders. And often enough
this game was played within the sides, as a number
of men manoeuvred for leadership. The chief technique was the political trial, and the chief instru-
mentalities were the dining-clubs and the sycophants.
These, too, I would argue, were structurally a part of
the system, not an accidental or avoidable excres-
cence. Ostracism, the so-called *graphe paranomon*,
and the formal popular scrutiny of archons, generals
and other officials, were all deliberately introduced as
safety devices, either against excessive individual
power (and potential tyranny) or against corruption
and malfeasance or unthinking haste and passion in
the Assembly itself. Abstractly it may be easy enough
to demonstrate that, however praiseworthy in intention, these devices inevitably invited abuse. The trouble is that they were the only kind of device available, again because the democracy was a direct one,
lacking a party machinery and so forth. Leaders and
would-be leaders had no alternative but to make use
of them, and to seek out still other ways of harassing
and breaking competitors and opponents.

Hard as this all-out warfare no doubt was on the
participants, even unfair and vicious on occasion, it
does not follow that it was altogether an evil for the
community as a whole. Substantial inequalities, serious conflicts of interest, and legitimate divergences
of opinion were real and intense. Under such condi-

tions, conflict is not only inevitable, it is a virtue in democratic politics, for it is conflict combined with consent, not consent alone, which preserves democracy from eroding into oligarchy. On the constitutional issue which dominated so much of the fifth century it was the advocates of popular democracy who triumphed, and they did so precisely because they fought for it and fought hard. They fought a partisan fight, and the Old Oligarch made the correct diagnosis in attributing Athenian strength to just that. Of course, his insight, or perhaps his honesty, did not extend so far as to note the fact that in his day the democracy's leaders were still men of substance, and often of aristocratic background: not only Pericles, but Cleon and Cleophon, and then Thrasybulus and Anytus. The two latter led the democratic faction in overthrowing the Thirty Tyrants in 403, and in following their victory with the much praised amnesty. The partisan fight was not a straight class fight; it also drew support from among the rich and the well-born. Nor was it a fight without rules or legitimacy. The democratic counterslogan to *eunomia* was *isonomia*, and, as Vlastos has said, the Athenians pursued "the goal of political equality . . . not in defiance, but in support of the rule of law." The Athenian poor, he noted, did not once raise the standard Greek revolutionary demand—redistribution of the land—throughout the fifth and fourth centuries.[23]

In those two centuries Athens was, by all pragmatic tests, the greatest Greek state, with a powerful feeling of community, with a toughness and resilience tempered, even granted its imperial ambitions, by a humanity and sense of equity and responsibility quite extraordinary for its day (and for many another day as well). Lord Acton was one of the few historians to have grasped the historic significance of the amnesty of 403. "The hostile parties," he wrote, "were reconciled, and proclaimed an amnesty, the first in history."[24] *The first in history*, despite all the familiar weaknesses, despite the crowd psychology, the slaves, the personal ambition of many leaders, the impatience of the majority with opposition. Nor was this the only Athenian innovation: the structure and mechanism of the democracy were all their own invention, as they groped for something without precedent, having nothing to go on but their own notion of freedom, their community solidarity, their willingness to inquire (or at least to accept the consequences of inquiry), and their widely shared political experience.

Much of the credit for the Athenian achievement must go to the political leadership of the state. That, it seems to me, is beyond dispute. It certainly would not have been disputed by the average Athenian. Despite all the tension and uncertainties, the occasional snap judgment and unreasonable shift in opinion, the people supported Pericles for more than two decades, as they eventually supported a very different kind of man, Demosthenes, under very different conditions a century later. These men, and others like them (less well-known now) were able to carry through a more or less consistent and successful programme over long stretches of time. It is altogether perverse to ignore this fact, or to ignore the structure of political life by which Athens became what she was, while one follows the lead of Aristophanes or Plato and looks only at the personalities of the politicians, or at the crooks and failures among them, or at some ethical norms of an ideal existence.

In the end Athens lost her freedom and independence, brought down by a superior external power. She went down fighting, with an understanding of what was at stake clearer than that possessed by many critics in later ages. That final struggle was led by Demosthenes, a demagogue. We cannot have it both ways: we cannot praise and admire the achievement of two centuries, and at the same time dismiss the demagogues who were the architects of the political framework and the makers of policy, or the Assembly in and through which they did their work.

3 *Democracy, Consensus and the National Interest*

"What is good for the country is good for General Motors, and vice versa." That now classic remark still provokes laughter and indignation; such frankness (some would say "cynicism") is not a normal stance among public figures. But is it untrue? What *is* good for a country? What *is* the national interest?

One may plausibly argue that, given the economic system under which we live, the national interest is advanced by the growing power and profitability of the great corporations. Were the General Motors organization to collapse tomorrow, the immediate consequences in unemployment, declining consumer levels and much else would be deeply felt throughout the nation. It is also arguable, in a contrary direction, that such short-term negative consequences are the necessary, unavoidable prelude to a radical restructuring of the economy—also in the national interest. The choice between these two arguments, which is also a choice between incompatible definitions of the national interest, rests on fundamental conceptions of man and society, both moral and historical, more or less fully articulated, more or less free from ideological distortion, more or less consciously apprehended. The chain of reasoning from these underlying conceptions to the practical decisions is very complex, full of traps, false trails and uncertainties. Not the least of the difficulties arises at points in the argument where values collide, for example between the cost in human suffering and the presumed future benefits of an action, commonly, but not always cogently, formulated as a clash between means and ends.

No programme of public action is immune from these difficulties. Consider the current favourite, the antipollution programme, surely, one would think, in the national interest as a matter of simple common sense. Who benefits from smog, from the poisoning of marine life in rivers, lakes and oceans? No rhetorical question that, however, for, if no one benefited, then the dangerous situation in which all developed countries now find themselves, regardless of political or economic system, would in fact not exist. The automobile industry protests that it cannot afford the palliative measures proposed in new legislation. The labour unions lobby against the "eco-freaks" in favour of continued development of supersonic aircraft because hundreds of thousands of jobs are at stake. If the antipollution campaigners hope to achieve more than emotional satisfaction, they will have to pass from moral indignation to practical answers to the practical objections. If it is the case that the giant chemical and industrial complexes cannot afford the costs of antipollution, then, given our system, the economic consequences will be felt by the whole society, not by the corporations alone. And the choice, I may add, is not one for expert decision, but for political decision.

I have no hesitation in predicting the outcome of this particular debate. Steps will be taken to reduce the blight, but within the limits of what the large corporations will eventually concede they can afford by shifting the costs to the consumer. Pure food and drug laws provide an obvious model. I pass no judgment about rights and wrongs in making that prediction; I am merely stating the implications of the fact that in all western democracies today, there is an unwillingness to jeopardize the existing balance among class or sectional interests. Outside France and Italy, there are no large, genuinely radical parties or pressure groups, and even in those two seemingly exceptional countries, the desire not to disturb the equilibrium, uneasy though it may be, remains powerful, if not overpowering. "Political relaxation and consensus," it seems, have become the overriding national interest.[1]

How are we to understand and assess this phenomenon? How deep is the consensus? How far is it the outcome of political apathy, and therefore one more weapon in the armory of the elitist theory? These are fundamental questions. Consensus is not necessarily a good in itself; there was consensus enough in Germany about the "final solution," if not unanimity, and no one requires unanimity for consensus. Good is of course a moral category, and, we have seen, moral goals are excluded by a powerful school of contemporary political scientists. "On the one hand," writes a prominent exponent, "there is a great deal of eagerness to deal with politics in moral terms; on the other, the insights of psychology and anthropology and of political observation have silenced the urge." [2]

Now if the link between political science and ethics has in fact weakened, then this is the first time in the west, in the nearly 2,500 years that have elapsed since the Greek discovery of politics, that mainstream theorists have argued not merely that political practice is usually amoral but also that politics have essentially nothing to do with ethics. The Sophist Thrasymachus, with his rejection of justice as a persuasive element in political life, is a very odd ancestor for modern theorists of democracy to have (though they naturally do not acknowledge him). [3] One need only call the roster from Protagoras and Plato to classical democratic theory to appreciate how astounding a revaluation of values is being proposed.

Furthermore, the claim is false that modern psychology, anthropology, sociology or political science give any warrant for the new stance. These modern disciplines have provided many new insights into the variety and limits of choices of action, into the complexities of individual and group responses to situations and ideas, but I am unaware of a single "insight" that can legitimately lead to the conclusion that, for the first time in history, we must "silence the urge to deal with politics in moral terms"; or of a single "insight" that forbids us to judge one course of action better than another not merely in technical or tactical terms but also in moral terms, in terms of more or less desirable goals. The insistence on "value-free" social or political science turns out, in practice, to entail "the most extreme of value commitments." [4]

Again I turn to a detailed historical consideration, this time of foreign affairs, and specifically of the most complicated of all activities in that sphere, namely, foreign wars. There has never been a war about which there was universal agreement that it was or was not in the national interest. Most of us would judge the wars of Louis XIV negatively on that score, the war against Nazi Germany positively, but I need waste little time in recalling that not everyone shared either view. The wars of Louis XIV do not interest me anyway, any more than the wars of the Roman emperors: they contribute nothing to an understanding of the problem of *democracy* and the national interest. But the wars of ancient Athens are illuminating. Classical Athens was involved in three major wars, each a watershed in her history. The first was the resistance to two Persian invasions of Greece, in 490 and 480 B.C. The second was the Peloponnesian War, against a coalition headed by Sparta, which began in 431 B.C. and dragged on to 404, when defeated Athens was compelled to dissolve her empire. The third, against Philip of Macedon, involved as much diplomatic manoeuvring as actual fighting, but the one major battle, at Chaeronea in 338 B.C., effectively marked the end of classical, democratic Athens.

Inasmuch as the Persian wars introduced the element of invasion by a non-Greek power, there is perhaps less to be learned from them about the national interest, and I proceed directly to the Peloponnesian War. Was it in the Athenian national interest to engage in such a long, difficult and costly conflict? The immediate causes are controversial—two large books have been published on the subject within the past two decades alone[5]—but there is no disagreement that the deeper, long-term explanation lay in Athenian imperialism, and that, though the Athenians may not have sought the war, they were not surprised by it and they were not willing to alter their imperial course in order to avoid war.

When the Persian invaders were expelled from Greece a second time, in 479 B.C., a third expeditionary force in the not distant future appeared probable. So a league of Greek maritime states was quickly founded to clear the Persians from the Aegean Sea. Under Athenian leadership, the league achieved its objective in half a dozen years, whereupon, predictably, centrifugal tendencies set in. The Athenians responded by force; no state was allowed to secede, more states were brought in, the league rapidly lost its voluntary character and became an empire of tribute-paying states, subject to increasing interference from Athens not only in foreign affairs but also in their internal arrangements insofar as the latter were deemed to affect Athenian interests. The material gain to Athens is easily catalogued: an annual income from the empire somewhat larger than the total public revenue from domestic sources, the most powerful navy in the Aegean and probably in the Mediterranean world, security for her vital corn imports (which were sea-borne), and a host of secondary benefits which always accrue to a successful imperial state.

However, modern experience has demonstrated that a mere financial balance-sheet of empire is no more than a starting-point for analysis. In whose interest was the creation and maintenance of the Athenian empire? Phrased differently, how were the profits of empire distributed? °

Some preliminary considerations are necessary be-

° In what follows, I am deliberately narrowing the analysis by excluding what some political scientists call "symbolic satisfaction."

fore this question can be answered. At that time, the
main fighting force in Greek armies was the hoplite
corps, a citizens' militia of armoured infantrymen who
fought in strict formation. Hoplites were expected to
outfit themselves at their own expense, and they received no pay other than a modest *per diem* while on
active duty.[6] Hence they were drawn from the wealthier sector of the population. The navy, on the other
hand, was a more full-time professional body of rowers
(with a handful of officers). During her imperial period, Athens maintained a permanent fleet of at least
one hundred triremes, paid for up to eight months of the
year, in addition to another two hundred in drydock,
available for service when required.[7] The rowers were
drawn from the poorer half of the population, and so
there was a neat, significant pairing, the wealthy and
the army, the poor and the navy.

The tax system had a similar, to us unfamiliar, balance. In principle, Greek states considered direct taxes,
whether on property or on income, to be tyrannical,
and they avoided them, except in war emergencies,
when they resorted to occasional capital levies from
which, at least in Athens, anyone whose property was
below hoplite status was exempt. Normal governmental
income was derived from state property, farms, mines
and houses that were let, from court fees and fines,
and from such indirect taxes as harbour dues. These
were substantially supplemented by what the Greeks

called "liturgies," obligatory payments made not in taxes but by direct performance of certain public duties, for example, by providing the choruses for the religious festivals or by manning and maintaining the warships, the triremes. Although we cannot do the sums, the liturgies in Athens clearly amounted to a heavy financial burden. In the fourth century B.C., the religious festivals alone required a minimum of ninety-seven annual liturgical appointments.[8] And again the poorer half of the population were exempt.

In sum, it was the rule in Greece (not only in Athens) that the rich both bore the costs of government, which included the substantial costs of the public cults, and did much of the fighting in war. And now we return to the question, in whose interest was the creation and maintenance of the empire? In terms of material interests, the short answer is that the poorer classes benefited, directly, visibly and substantially. For thousands of them, rowing in the fleet offered a livelihood, modest but not far below that earned by the average craftsman or shopkeeper, perhaps more valuable to the sons in larger families of peasants who could add their naval pay to the family income. Another large number, perhaps 10,000, were allotted land confiscated from rebellious subjects, and at the same time allowed to retain Athenian citizenship. Control of the seas helped guarantee an adequate supply of corn, the staple food, at reasonable prices, and that was a critical matter in a community whose home production could not meet more than a fraction of the need. There were also gains for particular sections of the working population, the shipwrights, for example; but I need not go further into such details.

The profits that accrued to the wealthier citizens are surprisingly less apparent. Given the character of the Greek economy, all such modern aspects of imperialism as the opportunity for the profitable investment of excess capital or access to raw materials produced by cheap labour played no part. There were no Athenian entrepreneurs to exploit tea or cotton plantations, to mine gold or diamonds, to build railroads or jute mills in the subject territories. A number of upper-class Athenian citizens somehow managed to acquire landed estates abroad, but that was as much an irritant to the subjects as a substantial benefit of empire. The empire boosted the commercial life of Athens and what we should call invisible exports, through the increasing presence of foreigners as merchants and tourists. However, a large part of the trade was in the hands of noncitizens, not of the citizens who alone made the political decisions, and no ancient author ever raises commercial considerations in this context.

We are therefore compelled to look for invisible, or at least not measurable, gains. One was surely the ability of Athens to undertake extensive, extraordinary public expenditures, such as the great building programme on the Acropolis, largely at the expense of her subjects, that is to say, without adding further to the already substantial burden of liturgies borne by the richer citizens. And the second was the attraction of power as such, difficult to assess but none the less real for being psychological, immaterial, rather than financial.

That is not all. It is a remarkable fact that Athens was free from civil strife, barring two incidents during the Peloponnesian War, for nearly two centuries; free even from the traditional harbinger of civil war, demands for the cancellation of debts and redistribution of the land. The explanation, I believe, is that during the long period when the full democratic system was fashioned, there was extensive distribution of public funds, in the navy and in pay for jury duty, public office and membership of the Council, as well as the relatively large land settlement programme in subject territory. For many this may have been only supplementary, not sufficient income, but the buttressing effect was what was needed to free Athens from the chronic Greek malaise, civil strife.

It is also remarkable that regular pay for public office is not attested for a single other Greek city. Again I believe the explanation lies in the fact that no other city had large imperial resources at its disposal: not even those cities who introduced or refashioned democracy explicitly on the Athenian model could therefore afford to go so far as to pay the poor for the active participation they were entitled to as a right. We may reasonably surmise that, in consequence, the extent of actual participation was very much less than in Athens; the corollary was that elsewhere democracy lacked the educational aspect stressed in classical theory.

What I am arguing, in effect, is that the full democratic system of the second half of the fifth century B.C. would not have been introduced had there been no Athenian empire. Given the financial and military burden borne by the rich, it is hardly surprising that they claimed the right to govern by themselves, through some form of oligarchic constitution. Nevertheless, from about the middle of the sixth century B.C., democracies began to appear in one Greek community after another, compromise systems giving the poor a measure of participation, especially the right to select officials, while retaining for the rich the greater weight in decision-making. Athens eventually shifted that weight, and the only variable that was unique in Athens was the empire, an empire for which the navy was indispensable, and that meant the lower classes who provided the manpower for the navy. That is why I hold the empire to have been a necessary condition for the Athenian type of democracy. Then, when the empire was forcibly dissolved at the end of the fifth century B.C., the system was so deeply entrenched that no one dared attempt to replace it, difficult as it was in the fourth century to provide the necessary financial underpinning.

Not all modern historians agree with this analysis, but I do not think any Greek contemporary had doubts about the close connection between democracy and empire. "Those who drive the ships," wrote the fifth-century oligarchic pamphleteer I have already quoted (Ps.-Xenophon, *Constitution of Athens*, 1.2), "are those who provide the power for the state." That this was a condemnation, not a mere description, is clear from the whole pamphlet, for example, from this more light-hearted, satirical remark (1.13): "The common people demand payment for singing, running, dancing and sailing on ships in order that they may get the money and the rich become poorer."

It was not the empire that our pamphleteer was condemning but the Athenian democratic system erected on its back. I commented earlier on the openness of domination in antiquity, a consequence of which was the absence of ideological cover, of ideological justification, of empire. Pericles, according to Thucydides (2.41.3), boasted to the Athenians that "no subject [of ours] can complain of being ruled by an unworthy people." That is as near to an ideological statement as I am able to find in the sources, about either the empire or the Peloponnesian War, and it will be conceded that it is not much. There was extensive tactical debate, but that is another matter. Perhaps not many would have been as brutally outspoken as the Sophist Thrasy-machus: "In politics, the genuine ruler regards his subjects exactly like sheep, and thinks of nothing else, night and day, but the good he can get out of them for himself" (Plato, *Republic*, 343B). But not many expressed the opposite view in foreign affairs, that there should be neither rulers nor subjects. It was no great step from the universal acceptance of slaves within the society to the acceptance of subjects abroad, to whom the slave-metaphor was, indeed, sometimes applied.[9]

The absence of ideology entailed two other nega-tives. There was relatively little black-and-white por-trayal, little of Sir Galahad leading the forces of light against barbarians who tossed babies on the points of their bayonets. Success or failure in the power game was a consequence of circumstances, in which superior resourcefulness and greater self-discipline were cer-tainly factors, but there was little need to go on to the wholesale moral disparity and disparagement that are integral to ideological justification. Nor was there much trace of what in Hegelian language is known as the reification of the state, with its consequent argument from *raison d'état*, *Staatsräson* (there is no unartificial English equivalent).

"*Staatsräson*," wrote Friedrich Meinecke in opening his standard German work on the intellectual history of the subject, first published in 1924, "is the funda-

mental principle of national conduct, the state's first
law of motion. It tells the statesman what he must do
to preserve the health and strength of the state. The
state is an organic structure, whose full power can be
maintained only by allowing it in some way to continue
growing; *Staatsräson* indicates both the path and the
goal for such growth. It cannot choose these at random. . . . The 'rationality' of the state consists in
understanding itself and the world around it, and in
deriving the principles of action from this understanding. . . . For each state at each particular moment
there exists one ideal course of action, one ideal *Staatsräson*. To discern that is the burning concern of both
the actor-statesman and the observer-historian." [10]

Although this is the language of German idealism,
the concept of *Staatsräson* has also had a considerable
popularity elsewhere, as in President de Gaulle's persistent reference to the duties of a "great nation." But
not among the ancient Greeks. When Aristotle declared
(*Politics*, 1253a19-20) that the *polis* (city-state) is
prior to the individual, he meant that in the framework
of his teleology: man is by nature a being designed to
live in the *polis,* the highest form of *koinonia,* community; that is man's end or goal if he achieves the full
potentiality of his nature. When Aristotle judged the
merits of a government by whether or not it governed
in the interest of the whole community, his canons had
nothing in common with modern arguments from *raison*

d'état. He judged the state by canons of justice and the good life; the latter accept the existing form of the state as the paramount political, even moral, authority, and then judge, not by moral canons but by a biological metaphor—organism, health, strength, growth. It is hardly surprising that Meinecke called Bismarck "the master of modern *Staatsräson*"; [11] for his school of political thinkers, the state often turns out to be equated with the elite.[12]

But if ordinary Athenians, leaders and followers alike, nevertheless supported the empire on material grounds, without the mystical underpinning of *Staatsräson*, what, one might be tempted to ask, remains of the vaunted Greek link between politics and ethics? The answer, if the imperial behaviour of the Athenians is judged solely by their own code, is that an ethical system which has a place in it for chattel slavery is not undermined by the imperial subjection of other states. The Greek concept of "freedom" did not extend beyond the community itself: freedom for one's own members implied neither legal (civil) freedom for all others resident within the community nor political freedom for members of other communities over whom one had power.[13]

The Athenians favoured, and sometimes even imposed, democratic regimes in their subject states. As in all great-power conflicts, smaller states throughout the Aegean area were under pressure to take sides, actively or passively, with repercussions on their own internal structures and, political tensions.[14] No doubt there was an element of political conviction, or at least sentiment, in the Athenian practice, but primarily it was a tactic, their version of the Roman "divide and conquer." They learned that the lower classes in these, often small, communities, not always strong enough to break their local oligarchies, might prefer membership in the Athenian empire as subjects and the consequent Athenian backing for democracy to political independence and the consequent lack of democracy at home.[15] If, as was probably the case, the wealthier citizens bore the cost of the tribute to Athens, then the "price" of subjection, in material terms, was very low for the *demos*. And, I may add, it was on the whole a successful Athenian policy, for they retained support, including military assistance, from many of the subject states more or less to the end of the Peloponnesian War.

How then does the observer, not the participant, who believes neither in the mystical reification of the state nor in Absolutes, the mythical objective observer who puts his own morals and values aside, determine whether any political action, past or present, was or was not in the national interest? He must begin, it seems to me, with the commonplace that all political societies, and certainly all known democratic societies, have been composed of a plurality of interest-groups, ethnic, religious, regional, economic, status, party or faction. On any proposed course of action, these groups may differ sharply, either over tactics or, more significantly, over goals. And when, as is often the case with larger issues, any or all of these groups are each faced with a conflict among their own goals, the difficulty of decision is much intensified.

Nothing brings this point home so brutally as a foreign invasion. Quislings, we must remember, were neither all aberrant individuals nor all paid agents; some represented interest-groups who decided either that the price of resistance was greater to them than any calculable cost of surrender or that occupation by the enemy was preferable to an undesired internal situation. Those Greek states who, backed by the sanction of the Delphic oracle, did not resist the Persians in the early fifth century B.C. were an early example in a set of different but analogous circumstances. Or, to take another kind of Greek example, those sections of the Athenian population who refused until it was too late to take the risks consequent upon an appreciation of the increasing power of Philip of Macedon, father of Alexander the Great, were not, or not all, consciously abandoning Athenian independence and freedom; they were allowing one set of values to lull them into a misjudgment about the threat to other values. Recent parallels come easily to mind.

The interest-group structure of Greek society, of Greek political society (the citizen-body), was a relatively simple one. There were neither ethnic nor religious divisions among them; there were no political parties with vested interests as institutions. There were possible divergent sectional interests, between the rural and urban sectors, and there were, above all, the divisions between rich and poor. For this last division the term "social class" or "economic class" is misleading. This was a society in which the majority were landowners, ranging from peasants with subsistence holdings as small as three or four acres to the owners of large estates from which they derived substantial cash incomes; in which most trade and manufacture were conducted on a family basis, again on a subsistence level, with only a minority of larger establishments or larger commercial enterprises, employing slave labour; in which such modern concepts as capital, investment policy and credit are inapplicable. I therefore retain the language that all Greek commentators themselves used, and speak simply of rich and poor.[16]

We have seen how in Athens these two sectors of the citizenry backed the empire, though from divergent, and even conflicting, interests, and how a sufficient consensus was achieved, save for a minority of unrelenting opponents, about the full development of their kind of democracy. We have seen, too, that the decision to engage in the Peloponnesian War was taken by the Assembly, which, we have no reason to doubt, constituted a fair sampling of the whole citizen-body.

When, in the course of the war, it was decided to make the bold strategic move of invading Sicily, Thucydides himself removes any possible doubt. His own accent may have been on the fear which prevented the minority opposition from speaking or even voting, but it is legitimate for us to shift the accent to the fact that they were anyway a *small* minority.

Insofar, then, as the mechanics of decision-making are concerned, the acceptance by Athens of the Spartan challenge to fight the Peloponnesian War might be thought to have been in the national interest. All the main interest-groups in the society participated actively in both the discussions and the final decision. That does not complete the analysis: we shall also have to consider whether the national interest was correctly assessed. But first I must underscore that I am not passing judgment on the values that entered into the Athenian determination of their national interest, any more than I approve of slavery when I insist that slavery and the best of Greek culture were inseparably intertwined.

Such "moral relativism" (as it is sometimes incorrectly called) may disturb, but it is the correct lesson to be drawn from the "insights of psychology and anthropology and of political observation." They have taught us, not that we must silence the urge to deal with our (or anyone else's) politics in moral terms, but that we must acknowledge that other societies can act, and have acted, *in good faith* in moral terms other than ours, even abhorrent to us. Historical explanation is not identical with moral judgment. If one has a mystical faith in the "organic" state, or if one believes in Absolutes, whether Platonic or any other, then one has a single standard on which to measure all political actions, past, present and future. But then there is no point to any historical analysis at all. Plato was unyielding on that: all existing states, he said repeatedly, are incurably defective; the just state, the ideal state, will be governed by philosopher-kings through their apprehension of the ideal Forms, not from a study of historical societies.

Nor are moral standards automatically registered in a plural society; morals and interests are not neatly separable. In a recent work on the United States and world order, by an acknowledged expert, we read the following in a section headed "What is the American National Interest?":

> Outside the circles of the Extreme Right it is no longer fashionable to attribute unique values and special qualities to the United States, its political style, its way of public and private life. The special qualities sometimes admitted are more often the object of derision than of praise. Yet, there *are* such values, and they demand protection in a world of very rapid and quite unprecedented change. . . . [Their] articulation constitutes the essence of my definition of the national interest . . . , an interest that appears both moral and feasible to me. . . . What are these values? In the face

of ever more potent governmental and private bureaucracies, soon to be reinforced with the perfection of automated data retrieval, I wish to preserve a large area for individual freedom from manipulation by government, corporation, trade union, political party, social club, suburban clique, and computer. In the face of increasing capacity for control over all forms of life—whether through weapons or drugs— I wish to affirm the need for maximum respect for human life itself.[17]

Individual freedom from manipulation and maximum respect for human life are indisputable values, but one may doubt that they constitute an adequate operational definition of the national interest from which to construct a foreign policy. Most of us will agree that significant moral advances have been made since the days of ancient Athens: chattel slavery has been abolished; hardly any one challenges the principle of popular government, of democracy; no democratic political leader would talk publicly about empire in the language of Pericles; material progress has made it hypothetically unnecessary to secure material and political good at the expense of subject states. Yet the twin difficulty with the national interest, first its determination and then its realization in practice, seems not to have been effectively resolved.

This contention is in no way controverted by the fact that political leaders regularly assert that their policies are in the national interest, alternatives not. They have done so throughout history, and I am happy to accept their "sincerity," as well as that of both their supporters and opponents. But the debate is normally conducted on the level of rhetoric, aimed at persuasion not demonstration, and therefore does not reveal the truth of the claims. Nor does their electoral success or failure.

Writing about the way bureaucracy now functions in western democracies, Henry Kissinger said: "The premium placed on advocacy turns decision-making into a series of adjustments among special interests— a process more suited to domestic than to foreign policy." [18] He wrote this disapprovingly, but many political scientists, agreeing with his description of what happens, would judge the practice positively, as being precisely what the democratic process ought to be. But which special interests? How widely through the spectrum of interests that make up society is the advocacy effective in reaching the decision-makers? What if adjustment gives far more to one interest than to a conflicting one?

There is a mathematical model lurking behind the word "adjustment" which seems to me wholly inapplicable to social issues. That is obvious in foreign policy: Britain was faced with the decision whether or not to join the Common Market, and the choice was either yes or no; there was no middle course, and such "adjustments" as the concession by the Common Market of a ten-year delay before the withdrawal of preferential treatment for New Zealand mutton and wool amount to only small concessions to opponents of the Common Market. One group of interests has won over another, and that is all there is to it. Similarly, to return to the Athenians, either they invaded Sicily or they did not; no meaningful "adjustment" is imaginable.

Also lurking behind the concept of adjustment among special interests is the more general concept of consensus. In an essay published in 1961, P. L. Partridge suggested that the "important contemporary controversies about rights or liberties . . . tend less and less to raise issues of great generality. . . . Is there not an all but universal acceptance of the belief that continuous technological and economic innovation, uninterrupted expansion of economic resources, a continuously rising standard of 'material welfare,' are the main purposes of social life and political action, and also the main criteria for judging the success and validity of a social order? . . . They are the 'built-in' criteria which render irrelevant and impotent any alternative social philosophy." [19]

There are a number of difficulties with this view. The first is the question whether it is sufficient to stand on such a level of "great generality." Belief in continuous technological and economic innovation and the rest seems to me to be not much more useful operationally than belief in individual freedom from manipulation. Even without an "alternative social philosophy" there is room for sharp conflict over the practices that will best advance continuous technological and economic innovation and a continuously rising material standard. The pollution issue offers evidence enough, provided it is extended beyond individual acts of self-denial (such as restricting one's diet to "organic foods") to hard political demands that would threaten the current profit calculations of large corporations.

A more serious difficulty emerges in a cautionary note Mr. Partridge appended to his remarks: "It is possible, of course, that the political and moral consensus may be more superficial than appears; and that there may be conflicts or frustrations growing in the deeper social soils that most of us are not sensitive enough to perceive." If we abandon the agricultural metaphor, we could rephrase this to say that it is possible that the consensus is only illusory, that "consistent societal values" are found, by and large, only among the small sector of the population "actually sharing in societal power." [20]

Thus, an important study of the political beliefs of American voters at the time of the 1964 presidential campaign revealed "not only a separation in but a conflict between their attitudes toward practical Governmental programs and operations on the one hand, and their ideological ideas and abstract concepts about government and society, on the other"; [21] between answers to such questions as, Has the Federal Government a responsibility to try to reduce unemployment, on the one hand, and, on the other hand, Has the government gone too far in regulating business and interfering in the free enterprise system? So sharp is the conflict that whereas sixty-five per cent of the sample (among whites) were rated completely or predominantly liberal on the "operational spectrum," the figure fell to sixteen per cent on the "ideological spectrum." [22]

The glaring lack of consistency reflects lack of knowledge, lack of political education, and apathy, but there is more to it. There is a very considerable element of political alienation when the issues are immediately relevant, and therefore more readily perceptible, as on local bond issues, which, in the United States at least, notoriously produce a large vote, and a large negative vote at that, especially among the lower socio-economic status groups, a protest vote not necessarily on the specific issue so much as against the "system" and against their own "lack of institutionalized civic power." [23]

The presence today of an ideological consensus, of agreement with abstract, general statements of "democratic" belief, is certainly not to be denied. The question, however, is the extent to which the "symbolic satisfaction" it appears to reflect overrides the deep frustration, accurately registered by the widespread political apathy, which arises from a feeling of impotence, of the impossibility of counteracting those interest-groups whose voices prevail in the decisions of government. "The costs of consensus are paid by those excluded from it." [24]

It would not have been easy for an ancient Athenian to draw the sharp line between "we," the ordinary people, and "they," the governmental elite, which has been so frequently noted in the responses of the present-day apathetic.[25] That difference in attitude follows from the fundamental difference not only between a direct participatory democracy and a representative, nonparticipatory one, but also from the difference in the interest-group structures of the two worlds and in the degree to which the various interest-groups have an opportunity to impinge on the decision-making authorities.

Finally, there is the question of whether or not the national interest is correctly assessed (apart from the divergence among different interests already discussed). On one level, there is the simple pragmatic test. Athens eventually lost the Peloponnesian War, and with it the empire. That is a *prima facie* argument for the view that entry into the war, despite the near unanimity with which the decision was reached, was not in the national interest. Of course, the argument cannot be settled that simply: one would also have to try to weigh the consequences of refusing to fight the Spartan coalition. And, in the nature of the case, the argument can be only an historical one; it can never be made by the actors themselves at the moment of taking a decision (or, for a considerable time at least, while acting in accordance with the decision once taken). On another level, there is the possible conflict between short-term and long-term interests, between the short-term interest satisfied by employment in the supersonic aircraft industry and the long-term consequences which, it is argued, are likely to be harmful even to aircraft workers.

This last point is carried to its furthest extension by Marxists, with their use of the term "ideology" to mean a false consciousness, a false belief about the interests of one's class. Some of the most sophisticated discussion will be found in the work of Antonio Gramsci; the central idea can be stated briefly, in a formulation by Eugene Genovese: "An essential function of the ideology of a ruling class is to present to itself and to those it rules a coherent world view that is sufficiently flexible, comprehensive, and mediatory to convince the subordinate classes of the justice of its hegemony. If this ideology were no more than a reflection of immediate economic interests, it would be worse than useless, for the hypocrisy of the class, as well as its greed, would quickly become apparent to the most abject of its subjects." [26] A simple example would be the familiar Marxist argument that imperialism and colonialism are contrary to the interests of the working class despite the immediate material gains that may fall to the workers of the ruling country.

In ancient Greece, with its open exploitation of slaves and foreign subjects, there would be little scope for ideology in the Marxist sense. Aristotle propounded a theory of natural slavery, according to which some groups of men were slaves by nature, others masters by nature; in consequence, slavery was beneficial to both alike. The doctrine, revived two thousand years later in the New World,[27] was hardly calculated to persuade the slaves as a group, and it proved also unpersuasive to the free Greeks, who abandoned it for the crude empirical view that slavery was probably unnatural but nevertheless indispensable and a fact of life. "Slavery is an institution of the *ius gentium* [i.e., of all peoples] whereby someone is subject to the dominion of another, contrary to nature" (*Digest*, 1.5.4.1).

In our society, on the other hand, with its much more complex structure and its formal abandonment of the idea that subjection and harsh exploitation are acceptable as such, there must be justification. If it is "self-evident that all men are created equal," it is also self-evident that all men are far from equal in independence, power, rights. Some explanation is necessary, and those who are not content with the prevailing explanations are certainly not all Marxists.[28]

Now, without a coherent social philosophy, a world-view, whether Aristotelian or Marxist or any other, the argument from the national interest becomes mere political rhetoric, an unanalyzable and untestable way of saying that what is good for General Motors or the Democratic Party or some other institution is good for the country. On the other hand, with a coherent philosophy, reference to the national interest becomes a tautology: the argument can neither be supported nor negated except by arguments for or against the fundamental philosophy which defines the interest, or by a tactical discussion seeking to determine whether a given action or proposal will or will not advance the larger programme required by that philosophy. Either way "national interest" is an obtrusive term that can only cloud the analysis, not advance it. Except in a very small, very simple society (the Greenland Eskimos perhaps) or in Utopia, the particular interests of particular interest-groups are the sole terms with which analysis can operate.

I have not taken up this much space merely to eliminate a bit of the rhetoric of politicians and journalists. What I have been attempting is a consideration from another angle of one of the themes of my first chapter, the place of apathy in the elitist theory of democracy. My argument is that, far from being a healthy necessary condition of democracy, apathy is a withdrawal response to the imbalance in the access of different interest-groups to those who make the decisions; in

other language, a response to "the development in
politics" which "has assigned functional primacy to
authority legitimation over interest articulation." [29]

I repeat my historical argument once again: If political apathy has not always been evident on such a
large scale in democratic societies, its current intensity
must be explained before it is either welcomed or
despaired of. Morris Jones hailed it as a "counter-force
to the fanatics who constitute the real danger to liberal
democracy," and Lipset specified the fanatics drawn
to "extremist movements": "the disgruntled and the
psychologically homeless, the personal failures, the
socially isolated, the economically insecure, the uneducated, unsophisticated and authoritarian persons at
every level of society."

Again there is the historical argument to consider.
Disgruntled, economically insecure, uneducated and
unsophisticated persons have always been with us; in
all preindustrial societies, in fact, economic insecurity
and lack of education were constant factors, the fate
of the great majority of the population. Why have such
people now become both politically apathetic and potential extremists at the same time? As for psychological homelessness and social isolation, it may be the
case that they were relatively much rarer in such a
community as ancient Athens or an early nineteenth-
century New England town. If so, it is as legitimate to
seek remedies for loneliness and isolation in our com-

munity-less society as to make a virtue of the loss of a sense of community.

What, finally, is an extremist movement? Under autocratic government, assassination and the coup d'etat are often the only available methods of bringing about major change in government policy. In a democracy, however, by definition the opportunity is continuously available through discussion, debate and selection procedures. A movement can then properly be defined as "extremist" (and we must recognize the looseness of the term [30]) not by the extent of the change it advocates but by its decision that conventional democratic procedures are ineffective for its purposes, that, therefore, methods must be employed which burst the democratic framework. Such movements were not unknown in the past, but in Athens, at least, it is not without interest that they were concentrated among the educated, economically secure upper classes, a few of whom did not flinch from assassinating Pericles' political mentor, Ephialtes, in 462 B.C., and from employing terror and assassination to bring about a short-lived oligarchic coup in 411 B.C.

That extremist movements have played an important part in twentieth-century western democracies is undeniable. What is the response of the elitist theorists? On the one hand, there is a certain Dr. Panglossism: this is the best of all possible worlds, and anyone who does not find it so has a clutch of epithets heaped on

him, personal failure, psychologically homeless, insecure, uneducated, authoritarian. "The quality which is
missing . . . is a quality of restraint." [31] On the other
hand, the theory is propounded that it is of the essence
of democracy that the opportunity to shape the policies
of government shall be narrowed to a periodic choice
among contending, decision-making politicians. There
is flawed logic in a doctrine which denies large sectors
of the population effective participation in the decision-
making process on the ground that their demands are
likely to be "extremist" and then seizes on their lack
of restraint as proof of the rightness of their exclusion.
"The grave mistake of theories on the urban slum,"
it has been well said in reply, "has been to transform
sociological conditions into psychological traits and
impute to the victims the distorted characteristics of
their victimizers. Practically, the unquestioned assump-
tion of slum irrationality has led to unrelenting prod-
dings toward self-fulfillment of the worst predictions." [32]

Allowance must be made for the possibility that any
given interest-group will abandon democratic procedures because they believe that they will be unable to
achieve their goals democratically. That was the case
with the Athenian oligarchs I have just mentioned, and
their belief was well grounded: given the Athenian
governmental procedure, they could not possibly have
won over the Assembly except by terror, assassination
and deceit. Our procedure is necessarily different, but

when the difference has reached the proportions which the elitist theory has converted into a positive virtue, how can a belief in the impossibility of persuasion be tested? The problem presented by this situation is extraordinarily complex and difficult. Historical inquiry, into both the recent and the more distant past, suggests to me that an attempt to resolve it by a retreat to apathy as a virtue is a desperate attempt to save the phenomena.

4 Socrates and After

"The object of this Essay," wrote John Stuart Mill in the introduction to his *On Liberty*, "is to assert one very simple principle, as entitled to govern absolutely the dealings of society with the individual in the way of compulsion and control, whether the means used be physical force in the form of legal penalties, or the moral coercion of public opinion. That principle is, that the sole end for which mankind are warranted, individually or collectively, in interfering with the liberty of action of any of their number, is self-protection. That the only purpose for which power can be rightfully exercised over any member of a civilized community, against his will, is to prevent harm to others. . . . The only part of the conduct of any one, for which he is amenable to society, is that which concerns others. In the part which merely concerns himself, his independence is, of right, absolute. Over himself, over his own body and mind, the individual is sovereign."[1]

There are notorious difficulties in trying to draw the line between conduct which "merely concerns himself" and conduct which does "harm to others" in the strictly private sphere. Mill did not make the task any easier when he bracketed "the moral coercion of public opinion" with "physical force in the form of legal penalties." Elsewhere in the same essay he insisted that protection "against the tyranny of the magistrate is not enough: there needs protection also against the tyranny of the prevailing opinion and feeling; against the tendency of society to impose, by other means than civil penalties, its own ideas and practices as rules of conduct on those who dissent from them."

Then he rather casually breached this pronouncement by introducing another distinction: "there are many acts which, being directly injurious only to the agents themselves, ought not to be legally interdicted, but which, if done publicly, are a violation of good manners, and coming thus within the category of public offences, may rightfully be prohibited." [2] And so we are plunged into the controversy over law and morals that is being so sharply debated today among theorists, legislators and the public at large.[3]

However, my concern is with the public sphere, with politics, and specifically with the rights (or freedom) of the individual in his political behaviour. Every state seeks to protect itself from being destroyed, from within as well as from without; states which acknowledge, in one way or another, freedom of expression then find internal self-protection complicated by the very existence of that freedom.

"Congress shall make no law respecting an establishment of religion, or prohibiting the free exercise thereof; or abridging the freedom of speech, or of the press, or the right of the people peaceably to assembly, and to petition the Government for a redress of grievances." No law? The liberal juristic interpretation holds that "the principle on which speech is classified as lawful or unlawful involves the balancing against each other of two very important social interests, in public safety and in the search for truth," and it "solves" the "problem of locating the boundary line of free speech" in this way: "It is fixed close to the point where words will give rise to unlawful acts." [4] The dilemma is the same as Mill's (and much of the language and argument are equally so). In the political field, the purpose of speech is to bring about action, and the proposed action may change the political system or the social structure so radically as to constitute a threat to the state from the standpoint of those who do not desire such a change. Who will then perform the delicate balancing act between freedom and safety, required by this definition, that will insure that both are preserved?

The dilemma is not restricted to democratic states, but will be found wherever the final sanction for political decisions and actions lies within the community itself, not in some higher authority. A divine monarch has no problems nor has a divinely sanctioned ruler, as was the case in the ancient Near East. There, as a distinguished Assyriologist, Thorkild Jakobsen, noted, "obedience must necessarily stand out as a prime virtue. It can cause no wonder, therefore, that in Mesopotamia the 'good life' was the 'obedient life.'"[5] Among the Greeks, in contrast, long before the introduction of democracy, the sovereignty of the community implied our dilemma: in the *Iliad* (2.211-78), Thersites was beaten and silenced by Odysseus for presuming to propose to the assembled warriors abandonment of the Trojan expedition, but that was because he was a commoner; any "hero" could propose freely, and from the viewpoint of the common interest, dangerously.

However, this example, and others like it, reflect a very inchoate community and therefore a rudimentary state of the dilemma, which then became central the moment the Greeks moved to a genuinely democratic community. In the first chapter I discussed two devices introduced by the Athenians in the fifth century B.C. in a conscious effort to cope with the problem. Ostracism was a device whereby a man was physically removed from the community for a period of years in order to prevent him from effectively expressing and circulating his political views; the *graphe paranomon*, a court procedure whereby a man could be tried, convicted and heavily fined for making an "illegal proposal" in the Assembly, even one that had been approved by that sovereign body, was still more ingenious: it invited a political speaker to accept the risks of his speech, should they be turned into action by the sovereign body, which clearly had the right to do so; it declared that a lawful act could, on a second discussion, be declared unlawful, its proposer punished for his words.

From these two institutions it might appear that the Athenians simply shifted the "boundary line of free speech" considerably further from the "point where words will give rise to unlawful acts." However, that was not the whole story (apart from the ambiguity in the term "unlawful acts"), and I propose to consider the Athenian experience in some detail during and immediately after the long twenty-seven-year war with Sparta, a war that had the explicit approval of all sections of the Athenian population, who believed that vital interests were at stake.

It scarcely has to be said that war puts the tension between freedom and safety to its severest test. In the United States, after the Alien and Sedition Acts of 1798, the doctrine that criticism of officials and laws could be punished as seditious was not revived until 1917, when the atmosphere suddenly became so charged that a federal judge could rule that, "No man should be permitted, by deliberate act, or even unthinkingly, to do that which will in any way detract from the efforts which the United States is putting forth or serve to postpone for a single moment the early coming of the day when the success of our arms shall be a fact."[6] Whether or not any court would repeat that today, politicians and editorial writers do, regularly, and much public opinion agrees.

How would the Athenian public have responded during the Peloponnesian War? Certain general distinctions have to be drawn before an answer can be attempted. To begin with, the two opening prohibitions of the first amendment to the Constitution of the United States—"Congress shall make no law respecting an establishment of religion . . . or abridging the freedom of speech"—would have been incomprehensible to an Athenian; or, if understood, abhorrent.

Greek religion was thoroughly enmeshed with the family and the state; a major part of the activity and the costs of government were devoted to religion, from the construction of temples and the organization of festivals, major and minor, to the preparation of the religious calendar and the performance of sacrifices and other ritual acts accompanying all public actions, military or civilian. The religion was polytheistic, by the fifth century B.C. quite complicated, with a large number of gods and heroes who had numerous and crisscrossing functions and roles, some imported from other cultures. It had little that we should call dogma about it, but was largely a matter of ritual and myth. In consequence, if the religion had the tolerance generally characteristic of polytheism, an adaptability that gave the individual considerable leeway in his religious preferences, it also looked upon blasphemy, for example, very seriously, as a public offence, an offence against the community whom the gods might hold responsible. Hence punishment was not left to the gods but taken in hand by the state.*

As for freedom of speech, much as the Athenians may have treasured it, and practised it, they would not allow that the Assembly had no *right* to interfere. There were no theoretical limits to the power of the state, no activity, no sphere of human behaviour, in which the state could not legitimately intervene provided the decision was properly taken for any reason that was held to be valid by the Assembly. Freedom meant the rule of law and participation in the decision-making process, not the possession of inalienable rights. The Athenian state did from time to time pass laws abridging the freedom of speech (one of which we shall consider shortly). If they did not do so more often, that was because they did not choose to, or did not think to, and not because they acknowledged rights or a private sphere beyond the reach of the state.

Account must also be taken of the Athenian court system, which was conceived not as an independent arm of government but as the people acting in a dif-

---

* It should perhaps be added that religion created neither pacifists nor conscientious objectors.

ferent capacity from their legislative one, and therefore through different, but comparable, organs, what we conventionally but very inaccurately call "juries" (a word Mill properly avoided in favour of the original Greek "dicasteries"). Court proceedings were essentially nonprofessional; that is to say, although there were rules of procedure just as there were substantive laws, the presiding officer was one of the annual city officials selected by lot; the parties were expected to make their own presentation, which was always oral—even documents were introduced as evidence by being read out—though they could obtain the assistance of experienced pleaders in preparing the case; the jury then arrived at a verdict, usually in a single day's sitting, by majority vote in a secret ballot held in full view, without any discussion. Basically the procedure was identical in public and private cases. There was no governmental machinery for bringing a man up on a charge of blasphemy, for example; that was the duty of any citizen who chose to take the responsibility, and who then conducted the prosecution exactly as if he were bringing a private suit over a contract.

In certain types of major public cases, the Assembly itself sat as a court, but normally large juries were summoned, selected by lot from a permanent panel of six thousand volunteers. (The number was 501 for the trial of Socrates.) Although we cannot say that the juries were a perfectly random sample of the citizen body—there may have been a disproportionate number of city dwellers, of the elderly, of the very poor who welcomed the small *per diem* though it was well below a minimum day's working pay—it is nevertheless understandable that the Athenians viewed large juries chosen by lot from six thousand of a total citizen population of thirty-five or forty thousand as sufficiently representative to count as the *demos* itself in action. There lay the logic in the *graphe paranomon,* in the notion that by this procedure the *demos* was taking a second look at a proposal, rather than that one branch of government, the judiciary, was reviewing the actions of another branch, the legislature.[7]

And there, too, lay a very profound distinction from our conception of a court. The role of the juries as the *demos* in miniature implied a political consciousness and a corresponding, to us unthinkable, latitude in arriving at a verdict. When Socrates went on trial in 399 B.C., not only would it have been impossible to find 501 citizens who did not know, or did not at least think they knew, much about him and his activities, and who had no opinions about him one way or another, but it would not have occurred to anyone that bland ignorance and even-handed tolerance might be desirable. Civic responsibility and fair-minded honesty in appraising the law and the evidence were expected, and every citizen of Athens was assumed to possess these qualities, when sitting on a jury as in the Assembly or Council.

After these preliminaries have been clarified, we are ready to examine Athens in the Peloponnesian War, and my first case study is that of one man, the playwright Aristophanes, a comic poet whose career as dramatist began at an early age, perhaps eighteen, a few years after the war broke out in 431 B.C., and continued long after its cessation, until at least 386 B.C. Of his first ten comedies, seven appear to have touched on the war, sometimes as the almost exclusive subject, in a tone that is hard to communicate to anyone who has not read Aristophanes. He was boisterous, outrageous, scatological, obscene, mocking, with an endless capacity for invention, and a genius for discovering humour and wit in the foibles of public figures, from Pericles down, in the qualities of the average Athenian, in the motives and conduct of the war, even in the familiar myths and rituals.

The first surviving play, the *Acharnians*, produced in 425 B.C., has the war as its sole theme, and in the final scene, the old peasant who is the protagonist makes his own peace with the enemy in a riot of nonsense, not all of it without bitterness. When Aristophanes selected other subjects, they were all equally public in their substance, and then in 411 he returned to the war, in the *Lysistrata*. That was a bad period for Athens: the Sicilian expedition had ended two years earlier in a great disaster; there was political turmoil; any hope of winning the war now appeared to rest on the financial support of the traditional enemy of the Greeks, the Persian emperor. So in his play Aristophanes has the wives of Greece, led by Lysistrata, an Athenian woman, conspire to force peace by refusing to have sexual relations with their husbands. On one level, the comedy is one continuous erotic joke, but there is a serious theme just beneath the surface, explicit enough in two passages (lines 1124–35, 1247–72), namely, that only the Persians can be the winners if the war is prolonged.[8]

To label these comedies simply as antiwar plays, as is frequent, would be to misread the situation. It is never easy to pinpoint the views of a great dramatist on the social and political issues of the day; the divergent judgments of Aristophanes among modern scholars make that clear enough in his case.[9] Yet one can see how Athenian leaders might have felt, in the words of the American judge whose decision in a 1917 case I quoted earlier, that Aristophanes should not be permitted "to do that which will serve to postpone for a single moment the early coming of the day when the success of our arms shall be a fact."

Indeed, Cleon, the most influential politician in Athens after the death of Pericles, tried to prosecute the still very young and not yet famous poet for his second play, in 426. Cleon failed, and Aristophanes

repaid him with some of his most insulting jokes in subsequent plays. The war was a popular one in Athens;
that is to say, victory remained the paramount objective in all sections of the community, not only in the
early, promising years of conflict but even after the
Sicilian disaster. The inference is that, despite Cleon
and presumably others, the freedom with which Aristophanes joked about the issues and the personalities
was not felt to be harmful to the war effort.

This popular judgment, uncommon enough in history, becomes unique when we consider the place and
method of dramatic production. Private theatre was
totally unknown. Both comedies and tragedies were
performed in competition, in an open-air theatre on the
slope of the Acropolis, only once or twice a year at the
major religious festivals conducted by the state. The
selection of the plays was in the province of the archon,
one of the officials chosen annually by lot; the costs
were borne by wealthy individuals through the liturgy
system. Each performance was therefore a major civic
occasion, sponsored by the state, patronized by a god,
Dionysus, and attended by more than 10,000 people.

There is nothing comparable in our experience, and
many remarkable features, such as the (to us) irreverence which was not merely permitted but was expected in a solemn religious celebration, are largely
outside my province. My immediate concern is with
the rough way the war was mocked, at a festival of the

state, not once but repeatedly, and not only by Aristophanes but also by other comic playwrights competing with him for the prizes. No one could have been surprised at the tone and the theme the second time or the third time, yet Aristophanes was selected as a competitor year in and year out, as if he were being invited to make annual sport of the people and their most vital interests. The phenomenon has no parallel known to me. In 1967, not a war year, the Board of the National Theatre banned the forthcoming production of a Hochhuth play. They were defended by Mr. Jo Grimond, former leader of the Liberal Party, in these terms: "The National Theatre is an institution of the State. One of the main functions of any State is to stop nonconformity." [10]

A concurrent development, my second case-study, appears to have taken the opposite direction. On the motion of a professional diviner named Diopeithes, the Assembly passed a law making it a major offence to teach astronomy or to deny the existence of the supernatural.[11] Neither the precise wording of the law nor the date of its introduction nor the details of the prosecutions that followed are certain. It was passed some time between 432 B.C. and 430 or 429, that is, either just before or soon after the beginning of the war, in the same period in which Aristophanes entered the scene.

The first victim was the outstanding mathematician-

philosopher, Anaxagoras of Clazomenae, not an Athenian citizen, who escaped punishment by leaving the
city. Anaxagoras taught that the sun was not a divinity
but, like the moon and the stars, a red-hot stone, and
that explains how the link between astronomy and
disbelief in the supernatural came to be made in ortho-
dox minds. He was also a close friend of Pericles,
which has led some historians to suggest that behind
Diopeithes stood political enemies of Pericles, attacking the personally impregnable leader obliquely
through his friends, but that seems to me to misjudge,
in modern rationalist terms, the force of ancient fears
of the supernatural. A more tempting suggestion is
that the law was passed after plague struck in the early
years of the war, killing one third of the citizen body
in a four-year period.[12] Nothing arouses mass dread so
much as plague and earthquake, or provokes such
blind, violent response, still in many parts of the world
today.

Whatever the truth about these details, the broad
outlines of the unhappy story are clear enough. Sacrilege and blasphemy were old crimes, but now, for a
full generation—the trial of Socrates in 399 B.C. was the
final act—men were prosecuted and punished not for
overt acts of impiety but for their ideas, for statements
they made even when not accompanied by any action
interfering with the orderly conduct of religion. The
few men who, according to a not very reliable later

tradition, are said to have been victims were, without
exception, distinguished intellectuals. This may be accident—only the more famous names were remembered
—but I doubt it; the whole story has the air of an
attack on a sector of the intellectuals, at a time when
a number of them were questioning, and often chal-
lenging, deeply rooted traditional beliefs, in religion,
ethics and politics, a time of war at that. Aristophanes
joined the attack in one play, the *Clouds;* the playwright who stretched freedom of speech to the limit
in one sphere thus helped undermine that same freedom in another area.

Then came the morning in 415 B.C., shortly before
the great armada was to sail against Sicily, when the
Athenians woke to learn that during the night the
sacred herms had been mutilated in many quarters of
the city.[13] A herm was a stone pillar, normally smooth
except for a carved head and erect phallus, with an
apotropaic function, the warding off of evil. Herms
were numerous, at city-gates, on street-corners, in front
of public buildings and private houses. Just what happened during that one night in 415 is now buried beneath the public outcry and witch-hunt that ensued.
The action was too carefully and conspiratorially
planned for a prank or an ordinary act of vandalism.
A substantial number of people were deliberately creating a scandal for ulterior purposes, and, as I read
the surviving evidence, the organizers came from the

upper-class dining clubs of Athens, abetted by their hangers-on and slaves—a nice example of the "extremism" of the educated wealthier citizens I mentioned in a previous chapter.

One may also infer, but not demonstrate, that their objective was to thwart, or at least disturb, the coming Sicilian expedition. The chief victim of the double sacrilege was Alcibiades, one of the three generals in command of the expedition and its strongest advocate, who had hardly reached the island when he was summoned back to stand trial for impiety. Popular feeling ran understandably high: sacrilege on such a scale was rare and very dangerous; in wartime the consequences for the city could be total disaster, should the gods avenge themselves with the savagery they were known to be capable of. Prompt action was taken: there were investigations and trials, in an atmosphere of religious dread tinged with patriotic fervour; many fled or were put to death and had their property confiscated,[14] some no doubt the victims of private acts of vengeance in a situation not conducive to calm judicial proceedings; the repercussions were still being felt nearly two decades later.

The conspirators had obviously succeeded in creating a considerable disturbance, but not, if that was their intention, of sabotaging the expedition (unless it can be demonstrated that the absence of Alcibiades from the field was the factor that divided success from failure). Understandably, Alcibiades did not return to Athens to stand trial. Less understandably, he fled to Sparta of all places, where he was first received with suspicion until he persuaded the Spartans that he was not an Athenian secret agent but a patriotic Athenian whose country had betrayed him. He seems then to have served Sparta as an adviser for two or three years until he had to flee again, this time for no more serious reason than an alleged adulterous affair with the wife of one of the two Spartan kings. His next haven was in territory under Persian rule—Persia, it will be remembered was not at that moment an enemy—from which he was recalled in 411 to take charge of the Athenian military programme once more. Neither his conviction *in absentia* of sacrilege nor his traitorous relations with Sparta stood in the way under the peculiar circumstances of that year.

The circumstances were these. One consequence of the loss of virtually the whole Athenian army and navy that had gone to Sicily was the emergence of a careful plot to replace democracy at home by an oligarchy. The leaders, men of ability and standing in the community, achieved their goal by a mixture of terrorism and propaganda, not by open attack on democracy in principle, which would have been ineffective, but by a complicated patriotic argument. The only way remaining to win the war, they broadcast, was through massive financial support from Persia, and the king

demanded, as the conditions of his assistance, the recall of Alcibiades to supreme command and the institution of an oligarchic regime. The conspirators were
helped by the fact that the fleet was then based not at
Athens but on the island of Samos, off the Turkish
coast, so that several thousand citizens impervious to
their propaganda could not attend meetings of the
Assembly.

And so in 411 the Assembly voted the democracy
out of existence and a temporary Council of 400 into
power to prepare the new structure of government.
Within a few months, it became apparent that the
leaders of the coup were preparing to open the gates
to Sparta, end the war and retain power in Athens as
Spartan puppets. That not even the less enthusiastic
democrats were prepared to accept, and the cabal was
overthrown in a brief flurry of street-fighting. Alcibiades, who had not joined the cabal, was given the military command, democracy was restored, and the war
proceeded, for a time not too badly.

Alcibiades' last years and his pathetic end are not
my concern but the behaviour of the Athenian *demos*
once they were back in control is. They showed a
remarkable tolerance, failed to prosecute under a perfectly valid law that made it a capital offence to seek
to overthrow the democracy, and contented themselves
with punishing for treason the very small number of
men who were convicted of seeking to betray the city

to Sparta. They paid heavily for their tolerance a few years later. Sparta finally won the war in 404 and imposed a military junta, who came to be known as the Thirty Tyrants because of their brutality—among other actions, they murdered some fifteen hundred Athenians—and who included among their key figures some of the men responsible for the 411 coup.

Even the libertarian John Stuart Mill found this too much. Reviewing the relevant volume of George Grote's *History of Greece*, Mill wrote: "The Athenian Many, of whose irritability and suspicion we hear so much, are rather to be accused of too easy and good-natured a confidence, when we reflect that they had living in the midst of them the very men who, on the first show of an opportunity, were ready to compass the subversion of the democracy." [15]

The Thirty Tyrants did not last long. When the democrats threw them out after a brief civil war, they again punished only a small number and then declared a general amnesty. [16] That amnesty seems to have been well-honored, but it could not help Socrates, and his trial is my final case-study. [17] Several of the Thirty Tyrants were associated in the public mind with Socrates as intellectuals, but he was not brought to trial in 399 B.C. on a political charge, and therefore he could not plead the amnesty.

The indictment, read out to the jury of 501 men to open the proceedings, ran as follows: "This indictment

and affidavit are sworn to by Meletus the son of
Meletus of the deme Pitthos, against Socrates the son
of Sophroniscus of the deme Alopece. Socrates is
accused of not believing in the gods in whom the city
believes, and of introducing other new divinities. He
is also guilty of corrupting the young. The penalty
proposed is death." [18]

The wording as it has come down to us may lack
juristic precision and elegance, but there can be no
question that the charge was essentially one of impiety
and that it rested on the law of Diopeithes, now a
generation old. The man who laid the charge, Meletus,
acted in a private capacity, as I have explained, and
we unfortunately do not know enough about him to
help us assess the situation. He was associated in the
trial with two other men, Lycon, equally unknown,
and Anytus, a prominent and responsible political
figure with a career of some distinction and patriotic
service behind him. Anytus was reputed, among other
things, for his insistence on strict enforcement of the
amnesty; his participation is a guarantee that the trial
of Socrates cannot be easily characterized as mere
political revenge. Indeed, the political-vengeance view
is a late one; contemporary comments on the case did
not adopt it, no doubt because they had no difficulty
in accepting a trial for impiety at face value.

That is not to say that the recent political troubles
in Athens were not in the minds of many of the jurors.

They would have been very odd people if this were not the case, given the kind of close-knit community Athens then was and the extent of the troubles. But Socrates was not a political revolutionary, nor could he have been thought impious or a blasphemer in the usual sense of those terms. His trial seems not to have been accompanied by a popular outcry, unlike the affair of the mutilation of the herms fifteen years earlier. The vote to convict was close: 281 for, 220 against. It was, however, a vote to convict, and we must ask how it was possible for 281 jurors to find the deeply pious Socrates guilty of impiety.

The key, I suggest, lies in the charge of corrupting the young. What could that have meant? No direct answer is available because Socrates left no written work behind. We must infer from the writings of his associates and pupils, Plato and Xenophon above all, and they are not consistent even in their reports of Socrates' trial. Nevertheless, it is possible to delineate the background of the charge of corrupting the young, and to evoke the popular psychology, with a fair assurance of accuracy.

In their Apologies (the more or less fictitious accounts of Socrates' defense written in the next generation), both Plato and Xenophon stress Socrates' role as a teacher. There is a dramatic moment in Xenophon's *Apology* when Socrates turns to Meletus in court and challenges him: Name one man whom I

corrupted from piety to impiety. Meletus replies: I
can name those whom you persuaded to follow your
authority rather than the authority of their parents.
Yes, says Socrates, but in the matter of education one
should rely on experts, not on kinsmen. To whom
should one turn when a physician or a general is
needed, to parents and brothers or to those most
qualified by knowledge?

This interchange, fictitious though it may be, artless
though it may appear on the surface, strikes at the
heart of the issue. Half a century earlier, Greek schooling was still restricted to the bare fundamentals,
reading, writing and arithmetic. Beyond that level,
formal instruction was given only in music, athletics,
horsemanship and military practices. Men of the generation of Pericles and Sophocles learned everything
else by living an active community life: round the
dinner table, at the theatre during the religious festivals, in the town square, at meetings of the Assembly
—in short, from parents and elders, precisely as Xenophon had Meletus insist they should.

Then, roughly in the middle of the fifth century B.C.,
there came a revolution in Greek education, with
Athens as a centre. Professional teachers appeared,
called Sophists, who offered instruction in rhetoric,
philosophy and politics to the young men with the
leisure for study and the means to pay the considerable fees, to the sons of the wealthier citizens, some

of whom eventually became active partisans of the oligarchic coup of 411 and of the Thirty Tyrants in 404. Not that the Sophists were all antidemocratic or shared a common political outlook—Protagoras, as we saw, produced a theory of democracy—but they shared a common method of inquiry, which induced in some disciples a startlingly new attitude. All beliefs and institutions, they argued, must be analyzed rationally, and, when necessary, they must be modified or rejected. Mere venerability was insufficient: morals, traditions, beliefs and myths were no longer to be handed on from generation to generation automatically and unchanged; they had to prove themselves in the crucible of reason.

Inevitably such teaching was looked upon with distaste and suspicion in many quarters. A kind of know-nothingness developed as a reaction. In one of his dialogues, the *Meno,* Plato satirizes this attitude by putting forward Anytus, the most important of Socrates' prosecutors, as the spokesman of blind conservatism and traditionalism. "It is not the Sophists who are mad," Plato has Anytus say (92A-B), "but rather the young men who pay out their money, and those responsible for them, who let them get into the Sophists' hands, are even worse. Worst of all are the cities who allow them in and do not expel them."

Plato's irony is bitter. There is insufficient ground to accept this as a faithful statement of the views of

Anytus, but there surely were Athenians who did think and say just such things. Pestilence, oligarchic coups, mutilation of the herms—that is what came of these new intellectuals and their wealthy pupils, intellectually divorced from the mass of the citizenry as never before, men who did not hesitate to tear down traditional values, traditional morals and religion. It is mad not to expel them: this was no matter of abstract principle but a practical danger to Athens when it was already beset with troubles enough.

In Aristophanes' *Clouds,* in which Socrates' Thinking Shop is burned down in a typically riotous Aristophanic ending, much of the picture of Socrates is false, a conglomerate of the scientist-philosophers like Anaxagoras, of the Sophists and of comic invention. Plato objected angrily; we try to draw distinctions, too; however, the know-nothing attitude brushed them aside as irrelevant hair-splitting: the whole lot were corrupters of the young, and what did it matter if one corrupted with his astronomy and another with his ethics, or if Socrates refused to accept fees while the Sophists charged high ones? Aristophanes was surely playing on currently popular themes. Although he did not invent them, he intensified them, and Plato was right, I believe, to assign some responsibility to him, at a distance, for the eventual trial and execution of Socrates.

The distance from the *Clouds,* however, was twenty-

four years, and the question remains. Why was Socrates put on trial as late as 399 B.C.? Both Plato and
Xenophon imply that the answer is a personal one, that
Anytus and Meletus and Lycon joined together for
personal reasons which we can only guess at. Personal
grievance, after all, has been at the root of more than
one historic trial. The guilty verdict, however, is something else again: once the indictment was brought, the
long complicated background I have tried to sketch
weighed decisively against Socrates. There was apparently no strong desire to have him put to death: Plato
makes it clear that the old man was given the opportunity to go into exile and refused, preferring the
death penalty. And by then the baleful atmosphere
was thinning markedly, so that Plato was soon able to
establish his own school in Athens, the Academy,
where he taught without interference for a full generation. What Plato taught, I need hardly say, was hostile
in the most radical sense to traditional Athenian
beliefs and values. That is the crowning irony of the
whole tragic story.

We have not yet finished with ironies. For Plato the
condemnation of Socrates symbolized the evil of any
open or free society, not just a democratic one. And
Plato, convinced of the existence of Absolutes and of
the state's obligation to bring about the moral perfection of its citizens, was consistent throughout his
long life in his opposition to an open society. In his

last and longest work, the *Laws*, written nearly half a century after the death of Socrates, he recommended the death penalty for repeated impiety (907D-909D) —"Plato betrayed Socrates" was Sir Karl Popper's lapidary comment.[19]

Those who do not accept Plato's metaphysics have no right to parrot his judgments about Athens: the one is necessary for the other. Viewed from a less absolutist base, the freedom issue in wartime Athens proves to have been extraordinarily complex, symbolized not nearly so well by Socrates as by Aristophanes. The Athenians found no perfect solution; as I said earlier, to expect that of them is to measure them by a standard no other society has attained, an unhelpful procedure, to put it mildly. Nor, may I say once more, is it helpful to seek direct answers to our problems in a small, face-to-face community, a community resting on a large, unprivileged base of non-citizens and slaves. On the other hand, in a broad sense, the Athenian problem remains our problem.

Certain distinctions can legitimately be drawn from the Athenian experience. In the political field understood in its narrow sense but including war policies, the latitude of expression was very wide, not only in the early years but even in the last decade of the Peloponnesian War, when it was going badly. The Athenian citizens did not fear political criticism because they had confidence in themselves, in their own political experience, judgment and self-discipline, and in their political leaders, protected by certain restraining measures I have already examined. They lost this self-restraint above all in the area of religion and morals, but even there one can see important distinctions. Public reactions depended at least in part on the occasion and manner of expression. Aristophanes and the other comic poets were free with irreverent jokes about the gods in a way that, in the mouths of philosophers or Sophists, could lead to an indictment for impiety.

The explanation, I suggest, will be found in the fact that Aristophanes' jokes were within the conventions of the religious festivals (like the rude jokes in medieval miracle plays), at which the community celebrated its gods, whereas the philosophers were neither joking nor functioning within the framework of the community; they were attacking it, or so many thought. Even the gods laughed when the protagonist in Aristophanes' *Peace* chose a large dung-beetle as the vehicle for his ascent to their abode. But no one laughed when Anaxagoras taught that the sun was merely a distant, red-hot stone. That was not intended as a joke.

Anaxagoras should not be underestimated, as symbol as well as philosopher. Plato performed the most successful illusionist trick in history when he persuaded posterity that the trial of Socrates was unique among prosecutions under the law of Diopeithes, indeed among all events in Athenian history. But what did contemporary Athenians who were not the master's disciples think? We must judge from silence, and, as I have already suggested, I see no reason to believe that Socrates stood out in the public mind as all that different from Anaxagoras or the other intellectuals caught up in the series of impiety trials. Like Anaxagoras, he could have escaped the death penalty by going into exile. Unlike Anaxagoras, however, he was an Athenian citizen for whom exile would have had different overtones. Anaxagoras was able to retire to Lampsacus in his native Asia Minor, where he was received with honours, and that raises a difficult question. The generation of the Peloponnesian War witnessed an assault on intellectuals and their freedom that appears to have been restricted to Athens, the cultural centre of the Greek world without a rival. How can we explain the paradox?

A favourite explanation among modern commentators places the responsibility on the people, the *demos*, uneducated, irrational, endowed with power they were incapable of using responsibly, the prey of demagogues. What is the evidence for this view, for which there is no ancient authority? I am aware of none. That the *demos* passed the law of Diopeithes in the Assembly is of course true, and it is equally true that the *demos* in the courts voted a number of convictions. But where was the initiative? The roles of

Aristophanes and Anytus in the Socrates case suggest that it came at least as much from the circles of the intellectual and political elite of Athens as from the lower classes, and perhaps largely from the elite. If that is right, then the series of trials, from that of Anaxagoras to that of Socrates, is as much a condemnation of leaders in a democracy as of followers, and this conclusion gets us nowhere, since autocratic and oligarchic regimes throughout history have not been excessively tolerant of ideas either.

I suggest that in this discussion historians have been too obsessed with form, not sufficiently alert to substance. Behind intolerance there is always fear, regardless of the form of government under which the repression takes place. What were Athenians afraid of in the last third of the fifth century B.C., enough Athenians to secure convictions and punishments? The answer seems to me to be fear of the loss of a way of life that had been built up in the course of a half-century, which had as its foundation the empire and the democracy; a way of life that was materially prosperous (in ancient Greek terms) and at the same time psychologically and culturally satisfying and, so to speak, self-satisfied; a way of life that was being tested and threatened in a long, difficult war; a way of life that also required the benevolence, or at least the neutrality, of the gods.

On the fighting front, Athenian morale remained

high; on the political front, too, as we saw in considering freedom of political expression. Little fear was to
be seen in those areas. The fear reflected in the law
of Diopeithes and the consequent trials must be identi-
fied at face value: fear that the moral and religious
fibre of the community was being undermined, through
the corruption of the young, and particularly, of the
young among the social elite.

The struggle was in fact being carried on within a
small circle, the circle from which leadership in the
community had traditionally been drawn. It was
young aristocrats who organized a club called the
Kakodaimonistai (literally, devil-worshippers), whose
programme was to mock at superstition and tempt the
gods by dining on unlucky days. It was men from the
upper classes who were the moving spirits in the
mutilation of the herms, who alone could afford the
fees charged by the Sophists for higher education,
who, Plato had Socrates admit in his *Apology* (23C),
were his young followers. It was from among these
same men that the oligarchic coup of 411 was engi-
neered, and then the regime of the Thirty Tyrants.
Can we really be surprised that there was a harsh
reaction, much as we may disapprove the forms that
reaction took?

Athens lost the war and the empire but recovered
her democracy, and, within a few years, self-confidence.
The fears evaporated. Fourth-century Athens lacked

the exuberance of the previous century; comedy remained a symbol: no longer did the playwrights construct their dramas round the great political issues of
the day or round the main public figures; they turned
instead to the quieter themes of money and domestic
life. But political debate remained open and fierce,
democracy unchallenged as a system, while the philosophers freely condemned it and taught alternative
political and ethical ideas. When Athenian democracy
was finally destroyed, the blow came from superior
external force, from Philip of Macedon and his son,
Alexander.

A genuinely political society, in which discussion and
debate are an essential technique, is a society full of
risks. It is inevitable that, from time to time, the
debate will move from tactics to fundamentals, that
there will be a challenge not merely to the immediate
policies of those who hold the governmental power
but to the underlying principles, that there will be a
radical challenge. That is not only inevitable, it is
desirable. It is also inevitable that those interest-groups
who prefer the status quo will resist the challenge,
among other means by appealing to traditional, deeply
rooted beliefs, myths, values, by playing on (and even
summoning up) fears.

The dangers are well known; impiety trials are but
one manifestation. "Eternal vigilance is the price of
liberty." No doubt, but like all truisms, this one offers

little practical guidance. Vigilance against whom? One answer, we have seen, is to rest one's defences on public apathy, on the politician as hero. I have tried to argue that this is a way of preserving liberty by castrating it, that there is more hope in a return to the classical concept of governance as a continued effort in mass education. There will still be mistakes, tragedies, trials for impiety, but there may also be a return from widespread alienation to a genuine sense of community. The conviction of Socrates is not the whole story of freedom in Athens.

5 *Censorship in Classical Antiquity*

The semantic field of the word "censorship" tends to be a narrow one today, and its emotional overtone is negative. The narrowness is enshrined in the *Oxford English Dictionary* (though not the pejorative tone). All that my 1955 edition of the *Shorter OED* has to say is: "The office or function of a censor; official supervision." And under "censor" there are four entries: 1) the Roman official of that name, and in a transferred sense, "one who has the supervision of the conduct of a body of people as in some colleges"; 2) an official who inspects books, journals, plays, and so forth or who censors private correspondence (as in wartime); 3) the "obsolete" sense of "a critic; a fault-finder"; and 4) the Freudian sense.

For the historian and the sociologist, however, this will not do on several grounds. A definition of "censor" and "censorship" is inadequate that has no place for either Mary Whitehouse (who is decidedly not obsolete), or the power of what anthropologists have taught us to call "taboos," or the possibility of manip-

A slightly revised version of a lecture originally published in the *Times Literary Supplement*, July 29, 1977.

142

ulating the law of libel or the law of blasphemy for purposes of censorship, or the economic restraints that may prevent publication and distribution of books, journals and so forth. The narrow administrative definition reflects the modern struggle against censorship by the state, and the libertarian ideology that developed in and out of that struggle. Even libertarians (apart from an extremist fringe) allow a margin of "legitimate" censorship and do not question the state's *right* to censor.

Nor is this a matter only of the state. I am thinking not merely of religious bodies, whom the editors of the *OED* seem almost to have lost sight of, who could and did censor their own members freely and frequently even when they had no political power behind them, but of "society," which inculcates and enforces taboos without reference to a police power. One need not be a Freudian to acknowledge the presence, and the necessity, of self-censorship. It is inherent in the process of growing from infancy into membership in a society, in the process of education, of being "civilized." As Sir Edmund Leach said in a talk in Cambridge, "A censorship-free social environment would not be a social environment at all, it would be a maniac's nightmare."

I am not proposing to embark on an inquiry into "unthinkable thoughts," but it is essential to appre-

ciate at the outset that they exist. So does fear of
knowledge. After all the allegorical and symbolical in-
terpretations of the expulsion from Eden and of the
Faust legend have been laid end to end, the original
conception survives; there are things that are best not
inquired into or known. In fifth-century Greece, that
remarkable century of "enlightenment," Pindar dismissed the philosophers and scientists for "plucking
an unripe fruit of wisdom," and, as E. R. Dodds
remarked, "the audience that saw [Aristophanes']
Clouds was expected to enjoy the burning down of
the Thinking Shop, and to care little if Socrates were
burnt with it."[1] Today the word "censorship" has a
pejorative overtone in intellectual circles that is far
from universal outside of them, and it was even less
universal in earlier epochs. Men consequently cen-
sored themselves, and, when they failed to do so,
official or unofficial intervention often received wide
popular support.

About the year 200, an Asia Minor Christian who
wrote an attack on Montanism apologized to his
friends in these words: "Some may believe that I
wish to add or append something new to the Gospels
whereas anyone who has decided to regulate his life
according to the Gospels may neither add nor sub-
tract anything from them."[2] That was of course written in the peculiar context of early Christian faith,
and it may be thought to be untypical, unfairly so.

However, all social and ideological contexts are peculiar (in the sense of specific) so that the unthinkable in one may be thinkable in another. In the early decades of the government of Rome by emperors, there were still influential men who were outspokenly republican. If they also happened to write histories, their assessment of the civil war which brought the first emperor, Augustus, to power, clashed with both "official" and "popular" views.

One of the early emperors, Claudius, was erudite and pedantic, and he pursued the practice, odd for a member of the imperial family, of writing lengthy histories. That was a harmless habit when he restricted himself to the origins of Rome and the Etruscans, but then he embarked on modern Roman history from the assassination of Julius Caesar. His horrified mother and grandmother finally persuaded him that he was in no position to recount the civil wars "freely and truthfully" (Suetonius, *Claudius* 41.4). So he began instead with the accession of Augustus. The imperial household provided an even less typical context than that of the early Christians, no doubt, but it helps to reveal the absence of universals in the subject under consideration.

There is, however, one valid generalization. Every social organism considers itself legitimate and assumes the right to defend itself both internally and externally; it therefore seeks to weaken or eliminate opposition, or at least some forms of opposition. The Athenians of the fifth century did not often kill critics of the system, as did the Roman emperors, but they sometimes ostracized them (in the technical sense of sending them into exile) and both methods were effective forms of censorship. Death remains the most certain way of preventing anything "immoral, heretical or offensive or injurious to the State" (in the *OED*'s language) from being propagated.

If the stress in our own world is on the media in any consideration of censorship, that reflects relatively recent social and technological changes. The invention of printing marks one historical dividing line. All older societies, even those as literate as classical Athens or Rome, faced qualitatively different problems with respect to censorship. There is an important sense in which it is correct to say that all written works in antiquity were a kind of *samizdat*, not because they were always, or even usually, illicit, but because their circulation was restricted to copies prepared by hand and passed by hand from person to person. Censorship of printed books and journals in advance of publication gives the writer and publisher the protection of certainty and relative immunity from punishment after the fact. *Samizdat* reduces the state's ability to prevent the dissemination of objectionable matter. The Roman emperors, lacking the resources of the modern police and secret services,

could not possibly find and destroy all copies of condemned writings, as Tacitus reminded them in his
account of the prosecution and death under Tiberius
of another historian, Aulus Cremutius Cordus (*An-
nals* 4.34–35). In his *History* Cremutius Cordus, a
mere senator, not an emperor, had praised Brutus
and called Cassius "the last of the Romans." Although
his writing was not the only ground for his prosecution, upon his conviction the senate—the senate,
please note, not the emperor—ordered his books to
be burnt.

Copies survived and were soon circulated again.
Tacitus exulted: "Alien rulers and those who imitate
their brutality achieve only their own disgrace and
their victims' glory." But, we are informed by the
learned Quintilian (10.1.104), when Cremutius Cordus's daughter began to recirculate copies in the
reign of Tiberius' successor Caligula, she suppressed
the passages that had brought her father to his death.
How long, furthermore, did the work survive thereafter? We do not know—we can rarely pinpoint the
disappearance of any part of the vast bulk of lost
Greco-Roman writings—but the fact that only one
brief, harmless fragment about the death of Cicero
has come down to us, and that in a quotation from
Seneca writing within four decades, suggests an
early disappearance.

I do not wish to make too much of this one instance. Someone has calculated that of the nearly 800 Latin authors known to us by name, more than one third are only names, perhaps 20 percent are represented today by at least one full work.[3] Often the lost writing warrants no shedding of tears; it is as imperative for society as for the individual that there be ample scope for what John Barnes once happily called "structural amnesia."[4] Furthermore, there were major temporary (as well as permanent) losses during antiquity itself. Juvenal's satires, for example, virtually disappeared for about 250 years after his death, and the scholar who brought them to light in the late fourth century seems to have worked from a single defective copy of the poems in Rome. Tacitus may have fared the same.[5]

Was any substantial part of these writings lost through pressure from emperors, senate and other authorities, irrespective of their literary or intellectual merits? That we are unable to answer; it is not a sufficient answer to enumerate works which were known to have earned imperial displeasure and to have survived nevertheless, such as the poems of Ovid, though it is certainly significant that this happened in a considerable, even surprising, number of cases.

Two facts must now be introduced about Cremutius Cordus and about the similar cases recorded by Tacitus and others under the earlier emperors.[6] The first is that they all occurred within the small circle of the imperial court and the senatorial class in the city of Rome. The second—which I believe to be a fact though it cannot be proved—is that no one intended or tried to seek out and destroy all existing copies of any condemned work, both because it was impossible and because it was unnecessary to do so. Voluntary compliance could be counted on, for one thing. Harnack wisely commented in his classic account of the survival and transmission of early Christian writings that, in assessing the disappearance of virtually all non-canonical works after the canon of the New Testament had been established, "one should not think of a deliberate plan, at least not in all but the rarest cases. The process accomplished itself more certainly through the instinct of self-preservation and common sense."[7] Besides, it really did not matter so long as the offensive words and ideas were not flaunted publicly in the wrong places or by the wrong people, or addressed to or in criticism of the wrong people.

Determination of what was or was not wrong, in all four categories, had a varied, complex history in antiquity. In both Greece and Rome, for example, there seems to have been no limit to freedom of defamation (as distinct from false testimony) in the lawcourts, as anyone knows who has read the Attic orators or the speeches of Cicero. This freedom was the accepted convention, not the result of legal enactment. In the theatre in Athens during the fifth century B.C. the same convention was applied—witness Aristophanes—and in this context the question of political censorship arises because every known political figure of any consequence came under fire, or at least ridicule, by one or another writer of comedy. Nor were the Athenian state and its policies any more immune than individuals. On this score a sharp divergence is noticeable between Greece and Rome; only one Roman playwright appears ever to have indulged in open political comment: that was Naevius, who is reported (in a garbled tradition) to have been in trouble at the end of the third century B.C. for having defamed leading aristocrats, perhaps the Metelli, "after the Greek fashion" (Gellius 3.3.15).

As for political pamphleteering, there were only two relatively brief periods when that form of writing assumed serious proportions in antiquity, during a few decades in Greece at the end of the fifth and early in the fourth century B.C. and during the final decades of the Roman Republic and the early Empire. In Rome much pamphleteering took the form of verses and songs, circulated orally, or of *libelli*, defamatory placards or broadsheets (whence our word "libel"). This practice can be traced far back in Roman history and a suit for slander was introduced as a retaliation. There is no way of assessing the frequency or the deterrent effect of slander suits, but it

is certain that in the bitter last decades of the Republic the most savage pamphleteering met with nothing
more severe than a counter-pamphlet, at least at the
level of a Cicero or a Caesar. Then came the rule of
emperors, and, beginning with Augustus, the offence
was brought under the rubric *maiestas* (treason), and
punished accordingly, if the butt was the emperor or
one of his closer associates. And with little delay, the
maiestas net was extended beyond defamatory *libelli*
to take in histories and other serious writings.

One may then well ask how it was possible for
Seneca or Tacitus or Suetonius to write and distribute
so many vicious comments and stories about emperors and courtiers. The simple answer symbolizes the
complexity of the situation: they were permitted, and
even encouraged, to defame any and every deceased
emperor, so long as they never broke the rule against
ridiculing the living. In that curious way each suc-
cessive ruler sought to add to his own lustre, by
the implied contrast with his unfailingly unsatisfactory predecessors.

There is no need to pursue this aspect of the subject further; one would quickly descend to the commonplace that freedom of political comment varied
with the nature of the regime: at its most extreme in
the Athenian democracy, more or less non-existent
under the tyrants or the autocratic Hellenistic and
Roman monarchs. The gradations and variations be-

tween the two extremes, however, are a barometer not only of the differences in political systems but also of fundamental social and social-psychological distinctions. The men who wrote the exuberantly outspoken plays in Athens and the men who acted in them were citizens, often of high status. Their Roman counterparts were not. Not even Naevius, a "Latin" from Capua who acquired Roman citizenship, could ridicule his betters as "part of a political activity of his own"; he "could do no more than versify the back-biting gossip of the rich and powerful men who gave him employment."[8] Playwrights of still lower status dared not even do that.

Nor was the freedom of defamation in the lawcourts identical in Athens and in Rome, if for no other reason than because the composition of the courts was not identical. When Demosthenes called Aeschines the son of a whore and Aeschines countered with "son of a slave mother," they were addressing the large popular jury-courts of Athens, with a membership that was a reasonable sample of the whole citizen-body. Rome knew nothing like them: Cicero's personal assaults were delivered either in the senate or in special courts composed of members of the senatorial and equestrian orders.

A favourite word in the Athenian political vocabulary was *parrhesia*, the freedom to speak one's mind openly in both private and public affairs, but especially in the latter, when it really meant the freedom of the citizen only. Critics of the democracy, notably Isocrates and Plato, predictably turned the meaning into "licence," "irresponsible speech," and their target was the status of the speaker as much as the substance of what he said. Learned Romans took the word over, but more often than not only in its pejorative sense, translating it as *licentia* or *comtumacia*. There is no proper Latin equivalent for *parrhesia* because, as Momigliano has noted, "the general attitude" in Rome, even under the Republic, "seems to have been that only persons in authority had a right to speak freely: one senses that freedom of speech belongs to the sphere of *auctoritas* just as much as to the sphere of *libertas*."[9] The Roman senate, accordingly, was an open debating forum, but it was very much unlike the assembly at Athens.

I have gone into the matter of political and forensic speeches because it helps us to locate the issue of ancient censorship properly, by diverting our attention from books and pamphlets. It is extremely important to realize that in classical antiquity (and indeed anywhere before the invention of printing) the number of books in circulation and the number of readers of books were infinitesimal and insignificant outside the small world of professional philosophers and intellectuals. And even they relied heavily on oral communication and memory, like everyone else. Books and

pamphlets played no real part in affecting or mould-
ing public opinion, even in élite circles. Of course
Roman emperors punished an offending writer who
flaunted his verses or *libelli* under their noses, so to
speak, as they punished an offensive remark at a dinner party. But they made no effort to seek out the
copies in private hands, not only because they lacked
the resources but also because it did not matter.
Nothing could illustrate the point better than the indifference of the triumphant Church to the continued
circulation of pagan writings (the occasional thunder-
ing of a Church Father or a Christian emperor notwithstanding).

It is inevitable, I suppose, that we today, and historians and other academics in particular, should over-
estimate the written word. Plutarch relates (*Nicias*
29.2)—and the story is at the least *ben trovato*—that
of the many thousands of Athenians who were cap-
tured at Syracuse in 413 B.C., a few were released
because they could recite some of the choruses of
Euripides. For the Sicilians, Plutarch comments, "had
a passion for his poetry greater than that of any other
Hellenes outside Greece. They committed to memory
the little samples and morsels brought to them by
visitors, and then shared them delightedly with each
other." Syracuse was no obscure provincial backwater;
its citizens were as literate, with as large a proportion
of men of high culture, as those of most contempo-

rary Greek cities. Yet they had to rely on oral transmission for the verses of their favourite dramatist
then at the peak of his career.

I have repeated this perhaps apocryphal story in
order to underscore the fallacy of much present-day
discussion of ancient literacy that narrows the question to the number or proportion of the free population (or at least the free males) who could read and
write. This misconception bears heavily on our understanding of censorship, and I shall therefore pursue it a bit further. To begin with, we must resist
the temptation to treat drama as exceptional because
even in our world few people *read* plays. All poetry,
and indeed all belles lettres, were commonly read
aloud and committed to memory, in snatches or even
(with Homer) in full. Otherwise they were unknown
outside a very small élite circle. That is why I have
regularly said "writings," not "literature."

And not only belles lettres were read aloud. Cicero
tells us (*On the Nature of the Gods* 1.23.63) that
when Socrates' contemporary Protagoras wrote an ag-
nostic work, he was exiled from Athens and his books
were burned publicly in the Agora. Other writers repeat the story, some introducing a new touch that
Protagoras was drowned while trying to flee. The
story is highly doubtful; Plato knows nothing about it,
and it is the sole reference in a classical Greek context to the *Roman* practice of burning books as a

form of official punishment. The story sounds more plausible in the version of Diogenes Laertius (9.54), that Protagoras read the offending work in public, perhaps at the house of Euripides. It remains dubious even then, but the greater plausibility comes from the accent on reading aloud in public: we remember, after all, that the one philosopher who was without any doubt put to death in Athens at that time was Socrates, and he never wrote a line.

When we turn from high culture—poetry and philosophy—to more mundane matters of concern to the average citizen, there is a similar misjudgment of the significance of literacy. Much has been made by modern scholars of the introduction of written law codes and of the practice in democratic Greek communities, notably Athens, of inscribing enactments, treaties, honours and other public documents on stone tablets, displayed in places in which people normally congregated. But, as Havelock pointed out, "one cannot build up a habit of popular literacy on a fund of inscriptions."[10] Ordinary Athenians did not have to wander about the city reading the texts of Assembly decrees or the laws of Solon. Their availability was sufficient; that is to say, they expressed the triumph of open government against secrecy and cabal. Mass literacy was irrelevant.

The classic Greek statement on the significance of written laws appears in Euripides' *Suppliant Women*.

Once they exist, says Theseus (lines 433-7, in the translation by Frank Jones):

People of few resources and the rich
Both have the same recourse to justice. Now
A man of means, if badly spoken of,
Will have no better standing than the weak;
And if the less is in the right, he wins
Against the great.

The struggle to achieve those codes took place in Greece in the seventh and sixth centuries B.C. and in Rome early in the fifth century, periods in which not even the strongest enthusiasts today would claim literacy to have been widespread. What was under attack was the aristocratic monopoly of the instruments of justice, heavily buttressed by their monopoly of knowledge of the law, which could not be broken so long as the law was nowhere recorded. The Roman Twelve Tables were the product of the plebeian victory in that struggle, but, as always in Rome, plebeian victories were incomplete. One of the measures included was the death penalty for publicly singing defamatory songs,[11] the only procedure available to plebeians at that time to express public criticism of their rulers.

In a society which relies on oral communication, the most effective method of censorship, short of the death penalty, is expulsion from the community. That is apparently what Socrates' prosecutors were aiming at, only to be thwarted by the victim's insistence on being put to death. Remove a man physically from his audience and the danger he represents is also removed; widely circulated writings require a different approach. In one of Plato's most ironic passages, he has Socrates' accuser Anytus complain bitterly that Athens did not expel the Sophists from their midst (*Meno* 92B). For its effectiveness, the irony requires that the proposal be a realistic one. Plato, I need hardly remind you, not only did not challenge the right of the Athenian state to prosecute Socrates—he merely denied the truth of the charges—but he himself, in the tenth and final book of the *Republic*, made one of the most massive arguments for censorship on record. Although his words are directed against poets, contemporary Greek culture and education as a whole were under indictment.

Expulsion or exile is associated in our minds chiefly with political opposition (or with certain kinds of criminal offence). Its use in this context in classical antiquity was common, ranging from individual opponents of tyrants and monarchs to the mass exile of whole groups of people in the frequent civil wars. We do not normally call that censorship, yet I would argue that, especially in a world of oral communication, it is precisely censorship, at least in those communities which were more or less open politically—

that is, open to debate over matters of policy. Anyone who was physically removed had no opportunity, short of armed uprising, to express and circulate his political views in the one place where they mattered, in his own community. Furthermore, as we shall see in a moment, expulsion of philosophers and prophets in antiquity was regularly justified by the threat they were alleged to constitute to public order and public safety. There was no interest in freedom of conscience; unexpressed words or ideas were of no concern. But there was also no serious support for that contemporary sophism which permits, or claims to permit, seditious words so long as they are mere words, not turned into deeds.

In 155 B.C., when heads of three philosophical schools in Athens came to Rome on an official embassy from that city and attracted much attention, especially among the young, the elder Cato persuaded the senate to order them to depart immediately on completion of their official business. One of the three, the Sceptic Carneades, head of the Academy (who, incidentally, remained firmly "Socratic" in never writing a philosophical treatise), took the opportunity to exhibit both his dialectical skill and his sceptical epistemology by giving two public lectures, one demonstrating the existence of natural justice, the other demonstrating the opposite, in the best Sophistic tradition. He lectured in Greek and one may doubt the extent of Roman fluency in that language, but the whole approach was intolerable. "Let them return to their schools," Cato said in the senate, "and practise their dialectics with Greek boys; Roman youths shall listen to the laws and the magistrates as heretofore" (Plutarch, *Cato* 22.5).

Six years earlier, some other unidentified philosophers had been expelled from Rome. After 155 B.C., however, no persecutions of philosophers in Rome are recorded until the series of executions and expulsions under the early Roman emperors, chiefly of Stoics, a few of whom were in fact politically troublesome in a vague way. How much of that century-long hiatus can be attributed to the fragmentary nature of the source material cannot be guessed; no one can pretend that we know even a fraction of the instances in Greek or Roman history. The suggestion is certainly plausible that the "absence of such incidents from the record of the years 155 B.C.-28 B.C. could indicate only that teachers of philosophy during that period took care to make themselves inconspicuous."[12] That the atmosphere in Rome had not changed is revealed by an analogous incident. In 92 B.C. the censors closed down schools of "Latin rhetoric." Their edict is quoted by Suetonius in the following words: "It has been reported to us that there are men who have introduced a new kind of teaching, and that the youth are going to their schools; that these men have assumed the name of Latin rhetoricians; and that young men spend whole days in idleness with them. Our forefathers laid down what they wished their children to learn and what schools they were to frequent. These innovations, which run counter to the customs and traditions of our forefathers, do not please us, nor do we think them right."[13]

The stress on "young men" had already appeared in Cato's assault on the Athenian philosophers in 155 B.C., and also, long before, in the trial of Socrates and in the diatribe against the Sophists that Plato attributed to Anytus. Young men who were interested, or pretended to be interested, in studying rhetoric and philosophy were all rich young men, drawn from the upper classes, as Plato had Socrates concede in the *Apology* (23C).

And that brings me back to an early point, namely, that what mattered was not merely the substance, the place and the persons propounding censorable ideas but also, and equally, the person or persons being addressed. In Socrates' Athens these rich young men were suspected of involvement in the partly clandestine anti-democratic clubs which brought off two oligarchic coups, in 411 and in 404 B.C. In Republican Rome, in sharp contrast, they were scions of the ruling oligarchy at a time when it is impossible, from this distance, to discern any threat to the structure of government or the locus of power. The fear was much looser and vaguer, but the censorship, including self-censorship, was more severe and effective. Cicero betrayed how profoundly Roman he remained despite his Greek erudition when he suggested that the punishment of Protagoras was an effective deterrent to later generations of philosophers.

There was another context, religion, in which the audience to be cut off from dangerous thoughts was a much larger and more representative one than the young men of wealth and class who drank up the words of philosophers. Before turning to that subject, however, there are two more aspects of what I might call "élite censorship" to be considered. The first is the narrow definition of "wrong places": until the later Roman Empire, the authorities, both republican and imperial, were content to drive out philosophers (as well as prophets and astrologers) from the city of Rome, or, in extreme cases, from Italy. In Cato's day, to be sure, Greece was still more a satellite than a part of Rome, but the emperors pursued the same policy, though by then the men they expelled carried on their activities quite freely in the Roman provinces. That did not matter: rich young Athenians or Alexandrians were still outside the Roman power world. Secondly, the prominence of "foreigners" among the expellees, especially under the Roman Republic, is irrelevant for our purposes, whatever its cultural implications or its convenience as propaganda for a Cato. Plato went out of his way to be explicit: "Worst of all," he has Anytus say, "are the cities which allow them in and do not expel them, whether a foreigner tries it or a citizen." And among the Stoic victims of the Roman emperors were senators of the best lineage.

I have for the moment jumbled executions and expulsions, as often happened in reality, but I must now separate them as we turn from philosophy to religion and cult. Polytheism is by its nature tolerant within broad limits; it does not face the same problems as monotheism with its exclusiveness, its orthodoxies and heresies. There were marginal areas in which the distinction became rather blurred, notably in the worry about the impact of "foreign" cults introduced into the community. However, until the appearance of Christianity no individual normally risked punishment for his religion among the Greeks or Romans unless he was charged with a specific act of impiety. Such behaviour as deliberate mutilation of a sacred image or scandalous mockery of religious rites raises few problems of analysis or interpretation. If we had any idea of their frequency, which we do not, interesting implications about ancient society might be drawn, but they would not come under the heading of censorship. They would rather fall within the category of taboos: the evidence is sufficient that prosecution and punishment by the authorities met with wide popular approval, when they were not initiated by public demand.

However, matters were not always so neat and simple. The justification for the punishment of impiety was that it either menaced the safety of the community or greatly offended public sentiment. Naturally, those in power determined what was a menace or an offence, and rulers and ruled were not always in agreement, as in Italy at the beginning of the second century B.C. The Greek mystery cult of Bacchus, which featured a considerable streak of maenadism, of ecstatic behaviour, spread rapidly through the peninsula; its followers were chiefly from the lower classes, especially among women, but also included middle- and upper-class members as well as slaves and freedmen. The Roman ruling class took fright: the senate and consuls marshalled a massive police operation to crush the cult not only in Rome but throughout Italy, even at the risk of violating the delicately balanced relationship between Rome and her so-called Italian allies. Thousands, we are told, were executed.

Traditional Roman distaste for anything not sanctioned by "our forefathers" is evident in the affair, not unlike that which brought the closing down of the schools of Latin rhetoricians a century later, but it can scarcely explain the scale and savagery of the suppression. Nor can impiety or even some weaker form of offence against the Roman deities: that much was conceded by the provision that individuals might still carry on the cult if they insisted, on application to the praetor and formal permission by the senate, with the condition that no more than five persons take part jointly in the ritual. That qualification provides the key. In all Livy's long and seemingly detailed account (39.8-19), filled with charges of lust, debauchery, forgery and poisoning—familiar enough in analogous situations both then and now—there is nothing of any substance to warrant the campaign of suppression. In the very first sentence, however, he uses the word "conspiracy," which he repeats frequently, hence the limit of five persons. And what was the supposed conspiracy? In a speech to the assembly the consul said, in Livy's words: "Until now their impious conspiracy is restricted to private wrongdoings because it has not yet the strength to seize the republic." In other words, there was no conspiracy, there was no threat to public safety; there was a large and growing mass activity, and that was enough.

Fear of unrest or turbulence, whether real or imaginary, turns out to underlie the entire history of official Roman actions against groups of people because of their religion (understood broadly enough to include the activity of soothsayers and astrologers), as distinct from the punishment of individuals for specific acts of impiety. The initiative could come from above or below, that is to say, the persecution might be undertaken by the government out of fear of turbulence, as we have just seen with the Bacchanalians, or it might follow popular unrest requesting it. The complicated history of the early Christians illustrates both possibilities. Until the empire-wide persecutions of the second half of the third century, under Decius and Diocletian, the attested instances were localized in various centres of the empire and regularly began with public hostility by Jews or pagans. The Roman government, it is important to note, was represented by provincial governors, reflecting a qualitatively different situation from the expulsion of philosophers from Rome and Italy with indifference to their continued activity in the provinces. The notable exception, Nero's persecution of the Christians in Rome after the great fire of A.D. 64, does not upset the argument: Nero needed a scapegoat to quiet the dangerous unrest in the city induced by the fire. With Decius the roles were reversed: the initiative came from the emperors, the population at large seemed indifferent when not actually friendly to the Christians.

The Christians, like the Bacchanalians and the others, were of course unofficial cult groups, but that is unimportant in this context. Throughout antiquity public and private cults coexisted. No licensing system, no registration or other form of official permission and control was required, unless the threat to public safety was alleged, as with the Bacchanalians. The story of astrology at Rome offers a neat (and my final) case study. The search for knowledge about the future was an integral element of ancient culture, in every period and at every level of society. Public authorities consulted oracles and soothsayers, and often had their own officials for that purpose, but simultaneously there were numerous individuals who practised privately as fortune tellers. Sceptics like Thucydides may have sneered at them, but their popularity and their acceptance by both state and society were universal.

There was also an unavoidable ambiguity about the soothsayer (witness Tiresias in Sophocles' *Oedipus*). Secret knowledge of what would happen was both comforting and dangerous, and the astrologers of Rome epitomized both aspects. Although every Roman emperor was a devotee, there were eight certain instances of the expulsion of astrologers from Rome (excluding favoured individuals, of course) between 44 B.C. and the death of Marcus Aurelius in A.D. 180, and there may have been half a dozen others.[14] Without exception, the ancient sources attribute the banishment to "turbulence," "rebellion," or "plotting." Again we appear to have the familiar expulsion from the capital only, but not quite. In A.D. 11 a law was introduced throughout the empire forbidding diviners "to prophesy to any person alone or to prophesy regarding death" (Dio Cassius 56.25.5). No doubt the opportunity for private blackmail required governmental attention, but that was a minor concern. In the fear-and-conspiracy atmosphere of the early Empire, an inquiry into the date of the emperor's forthcoming death was enough to set off a chain reaction, and the prohibition was soon extended to inquiries into the well-being (*salus*) of members of the imperial family.

This brings us back to my early question: how effective was formal, official censorship in suppressing ideas or writings? The leading modern authority on the astrologers at Rome noted that the emperors never "barred astrological studies and theoretical research." They "only interfered with the professional practice of the craft and that only in times of special political tension."[15]

That may also be said, with the appropriate modifications, of a whole range of disciplines. Mathematics, astronomy, biology, and other sciences proceeded without noticeable interference; if the heliocentric theory failed to gain support, that was not because the authorities denounced it but because the astronomers themselves found it unsatisfactory. Plato established his school in Athens within two decades of the death of Socrates and, so far as we know, it had an uninterrupted history of more than 900 years (until

Justinian closed all pagan centres of learning in 529) except for one brief hiatus. In 307 B.C., during one of the half-dozen desperate attempts to re-establish democracy in Athens following the death of Alexander the Great, a law was introduced requiring schools of philosophy to be licensed by the state. The measure was overtly political in intent: leading pupils of both schools, Plato's and Aristotle's, had shown an affinity for tyrants in the previous half-century. Nevertheless, the law was repealed in the following year, 306 B.C., whereupon Epicurus moved to Athens and organized his school there.[16]

No other philosopher attracted so much dislike and hatred in antiquity: Epicureans were occasionally expelled from Greek cities and from Rome; his name has become the Hebrew word for "atheist"; an anthology can be compiled of the familiar nasty charges of immoral behaviour and social harm. Yet the emperor Julian, in a letter consciously echoing Plato's plea for full-scale censorship, had to acknowledge the continued availability and circulation of the writings of Epicurus as late as the second half of the fourth century A.D. (*Epistles* 89.300C). As for the Stoics, targets of the early emperors, the crowning irony is that the last of them with a continuing reputation was Marcus Aurelius, the emperor in whose reign there occurred an unusually severe local persecution of Christians in Lyon and Vienne.

However, Tacitean exultation over the failure of censorship is not warranted. As the example of the astrologers at Rome reveals, censorship in the narrow sense was rarely exercised against writings, and then only if they contained a direct threat, real or imaginary, to a ruler or ruling oligarchy. This forbearance is not attributable to any notion of an inalienable human right of freedom of speech: no ancient state recognized so anachronistic a concept, not even Periclean Athens. If the state did not censor, that was only because writings as such were without sufficient effect. Teaching was another matter, and other forms of communication that led to "turbulence"; hence expulsion, not censorship.

Most often, genuine critical thinking evaporated in time anyway—if it came into being at all, as it rarely did in Roman history. Consider the Stoics once more. No authority compelled the chief spokesmen of the Middle Stoa, Panaetius of Rhodes and Posidonius of Apamea, Greeks living outside Roman control, to debase the original Stoic ethos to a comfortable accommodation with the rapacious and expansionist Roman oligarchy; nor were their successors compelled to adjust their philosophy further to autocratic monarchy. By then, as Brunt, more sympathetic to Roman Stoicism than I am, concedes, "rhetoric and devotion had largely replaced inquiry and argument."[17] Hegel said it with greater professional contempt in his *Lectures on the History of Philosophy*: "All speculative interest was really lost, and a rhetorical or hortatory disposition shown, of which mention cannot be made in a history of philosophy any more than of our sermons."

The classical Greek experience is more interesting, and more intractable. Although one should not exaggerate *parrhesia* in practice, since few outside the educated élite took the floor in political debates or attained (or even aspired to) political office and leadership; nor should one ignore the harsher realities underneath the Euripidean ideal of equality before the law; nevertheless fifth-century Attic comedy and tragedy remain as unimpeachable witnesses. Comedy in particular was a phenomenon without parallel to my knowledge: at major public religious festivals, managed and financed by the state, the playwrights were expected to ridicule and abuse ordinary Athenians and their leaders, the war effort and any piece of legislation that came to mind, as well as to treat the gods with an irreverence that few Sophists would have risked. Then, still in the lifetime of Aristophanes, a profound change occurred: comedy ceased to parade real people and withdrew altogether from its concern with public life. Why? The explanation certainly does not lie in formal censorship: no law forbade fourth-century playwrights from continuing the traditions of their predecessors. And nothing inhibited fourth-century orators in the assembly and the

law-courts from indulging in savage slander, without a
touch of humour in it.

The change proves to have been much more far-
reaching in the end. Dodds pointed out that "an
intelligent observer in or about the year 200 B.C."
would have been "painfully surprised" to be told that
Greek civilization was entering "a period of slow intellectual decline which was to last, with some de-
ceptive rallies and some brilliant individual rear-
guard actions, down to the capture of Byzantium by
the Turks; that in all the sixteen centuries of existence awaiting it the Hellenic world would produce
no poet as good as Theocritus, no scientist as good as
Eratosthenes, and that the one great name in philosophy would represent a point of view believed to
be extinct—transcendental Platonism."[18] The Roman
world, too, I need hardly add, with the exception of
a few great poets.

No more important and perhaps no more difficult
problem faces the historian and sociologist of culture.
Whatever the explanation—I offer none—it is evident
that censorship in the narrow sense was merely an
occasional off-stage diversion.

Notes

Numbers in brackets after titles refer to chapter and note where full citation may be found.

PAGES 3–7

CHAPTER 1

1. Common Cause, *Report from Washington*, vol. 2, no. 3 (February 1972), p. 6. See generally B. R. Berelson *et al.*, *Voting* (Chicago 1954); Angus Campbell *et al.*, *The American Voter* (New York 1960).

2. *Political Man* (Garden City, N.Y., 1960), p. 178.

3. *Political Studies*, 2 (1954) 25–37, at pp. 25 and 37, respectively.

4. Geraint Parry, *Political Elites* (London 1969), p. 144. It would be more precise to say that three chapters (21–23) of Schumpeter's book bear the whole burden of the argument. I cite the 4th edition (London 1954).

5. *Two Concepts of Liberty* (Inaugural Lecture, Oxford 1958), reprinted in his *Four Essays on Liberty* (London 1969), pp. 118–72; the phrases quoted appear on pp. 132, 134 and 145, respectively.

6. This defect in the theory that glorifies apathy has been pointed out by J. C. Wahlke, "Policy Demands and System Support: The Role of the Represented," *British Journal of Political Science*, 1 (1971) 271–90, especially at pp. 274–76. Surprisingly, Wahlke himself, in propounding a "reformulated representation theory" based on the concept of "symbolic satisfaction," reveals equal disinterest in the substance of governmental decisions. "'Low levels' of citizen interest," he writes (p. 286), "must now, if there is no other different evidence on the point, be read not as sure signs of 'apathy' or 'negativism'

173

but as probable indications of moderate support for the political community."

7. The English translation by Eden and Cedar Paul (London 1915), based on a revised Italian edition, has been reprinted with introduction by S. M. Lipset (Collier Books, New York 1962). I cite the latter.

8. See generally Parry, *Political Elites;* T. B. Bottomore, *Elites and Society* (London 1964; Penguin ed., 1966).

9. See J. L. Walker, "A Critique of the Elitist Theory of Democracy," and the irate reply by R. A. Dahl, *American Political Science Review,* 60 (1966) 285–305, 391–92; Lipset, Introduction to Michels, *Political Parties,* pp. 33–39.

10. Parry, *Political Elites,* p. 141.

11. R. R. Palmer, "Notes on the Use of the Word 'Democracy' 1789–1799," *Political Science Quarterly,* 68 (1953) 203–26, at p. 205.

12. Quoted from *ibid.,* p. 207.

13. Herbert McClosky, "Consensus and Ideology in American Politics," *American Political Science Review,* 58 (1964) 361–82, at p. 377.

14. *Political Parties,* p. 6.

15. Gaetano Mosca, in contrast, who had been a Liberal Conservative deputy until his (life) appointment to the Senate in 1918, pointedly reiterated his support of representative democracy after Mussolini came to power; see ch. 10 of the 1896 edition of his *Elementi di scienza politica* and ch. 6 of the 1923 edition, published as ch. 10 and 17, respectively, of the English translation, under the title, *The Ruling Class,* by H. D. Kahn, edited by Arthur Livingston (New York and London 1939), the proofs of which were read by Mosca himself.

16. Lipset, Introduction to Michels, *Political Parties,* p. 34.

17. *Ibid.,* p. 33.

18. Quentin Skinner, "The Empirical Theorists of Democracy and Their Critics: A Plague on Both Their Houses," *Political Theory* 1 (1973) 287–306, which he kindly allowed me to read in manuscript and which also gives an excellent review of the discussion. Cf. Graeme Duncan and Steven Lukes, "The New Democracy," *Political Studies,* 11 (1963) 155–77, at p.

163: "an obvious *non sequitur*, involving a slide from 'what we call "democracy"' to 'democracy'"; see also Peter Bachrach, *The Theory of Democratic Elitism, A Critique* (London 1969), pp. 5–6, 95–99.

19. Berlin, *Liberty*, p. 118, writing in a different but cognate context.

20. Not even that gentlest and least apocalyptic of prophets of technocratic doom, Jean Meynaud, has persuaded me otherwise; see e.g. his most recent *Technocracy*, trans. Paul Barnes (London 1968).

21. H. J. Mackinder, *Democratic Ideals and Reality* (London 1919), p. 243.

22. See Peter Laslett, "The Face to Face Society," in Laslett, ed., *Philosophy, Politics and Society* (Oxford 1956), pp. 157–84.

23. I have oversimplified and schematized, but without introducing any significant fallacies. Only the large juries require special comment in ch. 4.

24. These and related matters are discussed more fully in ch. 2 below; cf. Olivier Reverdin, "Remarques sur la vie politique d'Athènes au Ve siècle," *Museum Helveticum,* 2 (1945) 201–12.

25. Schumpeter, *Capitalism,* p. 269.

26. P. L. Partridge, "Politics, Philosophy, Ideology," *Political Studies,* 9 (1961) 217–35, at p. 230. Although this precise form of words does not appear in Schumpeter's book—the nearest is "democracy is the rule of the politician" (p. 285)—it is indisputably a correct summary. Earlier (p. 267) Schumpeter allowed that "there are social patterns in which the classical doctrine will actually fit the facts," but then, as in Switzerland, he continued, "only because there are no great decisions to be made." I need not comment on this pronouncement with respect to Switzerland; I need only say, as the next sentence of my text says, Not in Athens.

27. Reverdin, "Vie politique," p. 211.

28. The fundamental study is now H. J. Wolff, "'Normen-kontrolle' und Gesetzesbegriff in der attischen Demokratie," *Sitzungsber, d. Heidelberger Akad. der Wiss., Phil.-hist. Kl.,* Abh. 2 (1970).

29. The further critique of Protagoras in the *Theaetetus* is

on aspects of his teaching not particularly relevant to our concerns.

30. (World's Classics ed., 1948), pp. 196–98. Mill developed this argument at greater length in the first section of his long review of de Tocqueville's *Democracy in America* in the *Edinburgh Review* for October 1840, reprinted in his *Dissertations and Discussions*, vol. 2 (London 1859), pp. 1–83.

31. *Representative Government*, pp. 274–75.

32. Lane Davis, "The Cost of Realism: Contemporary Restatements of Democracy," *Western Political Quarterly*, 17 (1964) 33–46, at p. 40. Cf. McClosky, "Consensus and Ideology," pp. 374–79.

33. Schumpeter, *Capitalism*, p. 285, appreciated the implication of this innovation, more clearly than his disciples, I believe, but he of course drew different conclusions from mine.

34. "Domestic Structure and Foreign Policy," *Daedalus* (Spring 1966) 503–29, at pp. 509, 514, 516. The classic account is Michels, *Political Parties*, especially pts. I–III.

35. Kissinger, "Domestic Structure," pp. 514–18, has an interesting analysis of the implication for the mode of thinking of American political leadership.

36. See e.g. J. H. Lindquist, "Socioeconomic Status and Political Participation," *Western Political Quarterly*, 17 (1964) 608–14.

37. Andrew Roth, *The Business Background of M.P.s* (Parliamentary Profiles, London [1966]). For continental democracies, different only to the extent that large left parties, though not significantly less "professional" at the top, draw more leaders from the lower classes, see Ralph Miliband, *The State in Capitalist Society* (London 1969), pp. 54–67, with references.

38. Michel Crozier, *The Bureaucratic Phenomenon* (London 1964), p. 189.

39. "Domestic Structure," pp. 509–10.

40. Bachrach, *Democratic Elitism*, and Carole Pateman, *Participation and Democratic Theory* (Cambridge 1970), seek a solution in worker-participation in industry. Both thereby concede politics at the national level to the elitists, Mrs. Pateman being satisfied with the hope that the "ordinary man" would

become better equipped to assess the competing elites, Professor Bachrach abandoning the national scene altogether: "The main thrust of the elitist argument is incontestable. . . . participation in key political decisions on the national level must remain extremely limited" (p. 95).

41. Walker, "Critique," p. 292.

42. Lipset, *Political Man*, p. 403.

43. Davis, "Cost of Realism," p. 46. Cf. Leszek Kolakowski, *Toward a Marxist Humanism*, trans. J. Z. Peel (Evergreen ed., New York 1969), p. 76: "Right is the embodiment of the inertia of historical reality"; Alasdair C. MacIntyre, *Against the Self-Images of the Age* (London 1971), p. 10: The "end of ideology" is "not merely an ideology, but one that lacks any liberating power."

CHAPTER 2

1. *A History of Greece*, new ed. (London 1862) V 317*n*3.

2. Used only in 4.21.3, and "demagogy" in 8.65.2.

3. *Constitution of Athens* 27–28; cf. *Politics* 1274a3–10. A. W. Gomme, *A Historical Commentary on Thucydides* (Oxford 1956) II 193, points out that "Plutarch divided Perikles' political career sharply into two halves, the first when he did use base demagogic arts to gain power, the second when he had gained it and used it nobly."

4. Aristophanes uses "demagogy" and "demagogic" once each in the *Knights*, lines 191 and 217, respectively. Otherwise in his surviving plays there is only the verb "to be a demagogue," also used once (*Frogs* 419).

5. A. W. Lintott, *Violence, Civil Strife and Revolution in the Classical City* (London 1982), is unsatisfactory. One must still return to the inaugural lecture of D. Loenen, *Stasis* (Amsterdam 1953). He saw, contrary to the view most common among modern writers, that "illegality is precisely not the *constant* element in *stasis*" (p. 5).

6. See R. Bambrough, "Plato's Political Analogies," in *Phi-*

losophy, Politics and Society, ed. Peter Laslett (Oxford 1956), pp. 98–115.

7. It is developed most fully in his long account (3.69–85) of the *stasis* in Corcyra in 427 B.C.

8. *Politics* 1278b–79b; 1293b–94b; cf. Polybius 6.3-9.

9. Aristotle, *Politics* 1319a19–32; cf. Xenophon, *Hellenica* 5.2.5–7.

10. Pseudo-Xenophon, *Constitution of Athens* 3.1; see A. Fuks, "The 'Old Oligarch,'" *Scripta Hierosolymitana,* 1 (1954) 21–35.

11. *Athenian Democracy* (Oxford 1957), ch. 3.

12. E. A. Havelock, *The Liberal Temper in Greek Politics* (London 1957), reviewed by A. Momigliano in *Rivista storica italiana,* 72 (1960) 534–41.

13. *Aspects of the Ancient World* (Oxford 1946), pp. 40–45.

14. On attendance at Athenian Assembly meetings, see two articles by M. H. Hansen in *Greek, Roman and Byzantine Studies,* 17 (1976) 115–34 and 23 (1982) 241–49, reprinted with addenda in his *The Athenian Ecclesia* (Copenhagen 1983), ch.1–2.

15. See M. H. Hansen, "The Athenian 'Politicians,' 403–322 B.C.," *Greek, Roman and Byzantine Studies* 24 (1983) 33–55, and "*Rhetores* and *Strategoi* in Fourth-Century Athens," *ibid.,* 151–80.

16. See the valuable article by O. Reverdin, "Remarques sur la vie politique d'Athènes au Ve siècle," *Museum Helveticum* 2 (1945) 201–12; and generally my *Politics in the Ancient World* (Cambridge 1983), especially ch. 4.

17. A review in *The Listener* (2 Feb. 1961), p. 233.

18. Plutarch, *Pericles* 11.2. It was against such tactics that the restored democracy in 410 required members of the Council to swear to take their seats by lot: Philochorus 328 F 140.

19. See W. R. Connor, *The New Politicians of Fifth-Century Athens* (Princeton 1971), with the review by C. Ampolo in *Archeologia Classica,* 27 (1975) 95–100.

20. "Eunomia . . . the ideal of the past and even of Solon

. . . now meant the best constitution, based on inequality. It was now the ideal of oligarchy": Ehrenberg, *Aspects,* p. 92.

21. "Of the Populousness of Ancient Nations," in *Essays* (World's Classics ed., London 1903), pp. 405–6. Cf. Jacob Burckhardt, *Griechische Kulturgeschichte* (reprint Darmstadt 1956) II 80–81.

22. *Epistles* VII 325B; cf. Xenophon, *Hellenica* 2.4.43; Aristotle, *Constitution of Athens* 40.

23. G. Vlastos, *"Isonomia,"* *American Journal of Philology,* 74 (1953) 337–66. Cf. Jones, *Democracy,* p. 52: "In general . . . democrats tended like Aristotle to regard the laws as a code laid down once and for all by a wise legislator . . . which, immutable in principle, might occasionally require to be clarified or supplemented." The "rule of law" is a complicated subject on its own, but it is not the subject of this chapter. Nor is the evaluation of individual demagogues.

24. "The History of Freedom in Antiquity," in *Essays on Freedom and Power,* ed. G. Himmelfarb (London 1956), p. 64.

CHAPTER 3

1. Partridge, "Politics" [1:26], p. 222.

2. Judith N. Shklar, *After Utopia. The Decline of Political Faith* (Princeton 1957), p. 272.

3. See MacIntyre, *Against the Self-Images* [1:43], p. 278.

4. *Ibid.*

5. G. E. M. de Ste. Croix, *The Origins of the Peloponnesian War* (London 1972); Donald Kagan, *The Outbreak of the Peloponnesian War* (Ithaca and London 1969).

6. W. K. Pritchett, *Ancient Greek Military Practices,* part I (*Univ. of California Publications: Classical Studies,* vol. 7, 1971), ch. 1–2.

7. David Blackman, "The Athenian Navy and Allied Naval Contributions in the Pentecontaetia," *Greek, Roman and Byzantine Studies,* 10 (1969) 179–216.

8. J. K. Davies, "Demosthenes on Liturgies: A Note," *Journal of Hellenic Studies,* 87 (1967) 33–40. On the social psychological implications, see A. W. H. Adkins, *Moral Values and Political Behaviour in Ancient Greece* (London and New York 1972), pp. 121–26 (and pp. 60–62 on the hoplites and wealth).

9. See Russell Meiggs, *The Athenian Empire* (Oxford 1972), ch. 21, "Fifth-Century Judgements."

10. *Die Idee der Staatsräson,* trans. Douglas Scott under the title *Machiavellism* (London 1957), p. 1. I have modified the translation.

11. *Ibid.,* p. 409, note 1.

12. The same comment applies to "political realism": "Lacking more precise commentary, it loses all factual content and becomes a mere military watchword": Kolakowski, *Marxist Humanism* [1:43], p. 108.

13. See Finley, "The Freedom of the City in the Greek World," in my *Economy and Society in Ancient Greece* (London and New York 1981), ch. 5.

14. See e.g. I. A. F. Bruce, "The Corcyraean Civil War of 427 B.C.," *Phoenix,* 25 (1971) 108–17.

15. See de Ste. Croix, *Origins,* pp. 34–42; "The Character of the Athenian Empire," *Historia,* 3 (1954) 1–41.

16. I have discussed this point in detail in my *The Ancient Economy* (2nd ed., Berkeley and London 1985), ch. 2.

17. E. B. Haas, *Tangle of Hopes* (Englewood Cliffs, N.J., 1969), pp. 234–35.

18. Kissinger, "Domestic Structure" [1:34], p. 516.

19. "Politics" [1:26], pp. 222–23. Cf.: "In the Western World . . . there is today a rough *consensus among intellectuals* on political issues: the acceptance of a Welfare State; the desirability of decentralized power; a system of mixed economy and of political pluralism. In that sense, too, the ideological age has ended": Daniel Bell, *The End of Ideology* (rev. ed., New York and London 1965), pp. 402–403. The words I have italicized become crucial in the discussion which follows in my text.

20. Michael Mann, "The Social Cohesion of Liberal Democ-

racy," *American Sociological Review,* 35 (1970) 423–39, at
p. 435 (an important survey and analysis of the relevant investigations in the previous two decades).

21. L. A. Free and Hadley Cantril, *The Political Beliefs of
Americans* (New Brunswick 1967), p. 51.

22. *Ibid.,* p. 32; the summary table is reprinted in Mann,
"Social Cohesion," p. 435.

23. W. E. Thompson and J. E. Horton, "Political Alienation
as a Force in Political Action," *Social Forces,* 38 (1959–60)
190–95; cf. Mann, "Social Cohesion," p. 429 and Table 3 on
p. 433. S. M. Lipset and Earl Raab, *The Politics of Unreason*
(London 1971), omit this aspect in their summary (pp. 476–
77) of the Free-Cantril findings and in their own Conclusion
(pp. 508–15); they never consider genuine political impotence
as a possible factor in the creation of "extremist" attitudes.

24. MacIntyre, *Against the Self-Images* [1:43], p. 10.

25. E.g. Thompson and Horton, "Political Alienation"; Mc-
Closky, "Consensus" [1:13], especially Table VII on p. 371.
The assertion by K. J. Dover, in the *Oxford Classical Dictionary*
(2nd ed., 1970), p. 113, that Aristophanes' treatment of Athenian politicians "does not differ significantly from the way in
which 'we' satirize 'them' nowadays," has been refuted by de
Ste. Croix, *Origins,* pp. 359–62. Dover's more recent formulation, *Aristophanic Comedy* (London and Berkeley 1972), pp.
31–41–"the average man against superior authority," "the individual against society"—is no nearer the truth.

26. In *Red and Black: Marxian Explorations in Southern
and Afro-American History* (New York and London 1971), p.
33. He cites not only Gramsci's *Opere* generally but also
J. M. Cammett, *Antonio Gramsci and the Origin of Italian
Communism* (Stanford 1967).

27. D. B. Davis, *The Problem of Slavery in Western Culture*
(Ithaca 1966), pt. I; Lewis Hanke, *Aristotle and the American
Indians* (London 1959).

28. See Mann, "Social Cohesion," pp. 435–37. Cf. Free and
Cantril, *Political Beliefs,* pp. 176–81: ". . . the underlying personal political credos of the majority of Americans have re-

mained substantially intact at the ideological level. But the objective environment in which people live has obviously changed immeasurably. . . . There is little doubt that the time has come for a restatement of American ideology to bring it in line with what the great majority of people want and approve."

29. J. P. Nettl, *Political Mobilization* (London 1967), p. 163; much of ch. 6 is devoted to a development of this point.

30. Note the looseness of the "definition" in the section in Lipset and Raab, *Politics of Unreason,* entitled "Extremism: A Definition" (pp. 4–7).

31. *Ibid.,* p. 432 and *passim* thereafter.

32. Alejandro Portes, "Rationality in the Slum: An Essay on Interpretive Sociology," *Comparative Studies in Society and History,* 14 (1972) 268–86, at p. 286.

CHAPTER 4

1. (World's Classics ed., reprint 1948), p. 15.

2. *Ibid.,* pp. 9 and 120, respectively.

3. H. L. A. Hart, *The Concept of Law* (Oxford 1961); Patrick Devlin, *The Enforcement of Morals* (London 1965).

4. Zachariah Chafee, Jr., *Free Speech in the United States* (Cambridge, Mass., 1941), p. 35.

5. In *Before Philosophy,* ed. Henri Frankfort *et al.* (Penguin ed., 1949), p. 217.

6. United States *vs.* "The Spirit of '76," 252 Fed. 946, quoted from Chafee, *Free Speech,* pp. 34–35.

7. See the perceptive remarks of Bernhard Knauss, *Staat und Mensch in Hellas* (Berlin 1940, reprint Darmstadt 1964), pp. 122–28.

8. Cf. *Peace* 107–108, *Knights* 477–78, *Thesmophoriazusae* 335–38.

9. The analysis with which I am in most complete agreement is that of de Ste. Croix, *Origins* [2:5], App. XXIX, "The Political Outlook of Aristophanes" (with ample references to other views).

10. The *Guardian* for May 2, 1967. In the flurry of corre-

spondence that ensued, the Hon. Quintin Hogg, M.P., reminded me in the columns of the London *Times* (May 10) that the *Acharnians, Knights, Wasps, Peace* and *Lysistrata* "libel living persons and would today be restrained by injunction in the courts."

11. The only complete study of the Athenian impiety trials that followed the passage of this law is E. Derenne, *Les Procès d'impiété intentés aux philosophes à Athènes . . . (Bibliothèque de la Faculté de philosophie et lettres à l'Université de Liège,* vol. 45, 1930).

12. F. E. Adcock, in the *Cambridge Ancient History,* vol. 5 (1927), p. 478.

13. In what follows I am ignoring the contemporary scandal surrounding the "profanation" of the mystery-cult of Demeter at Eleusis, which, rather than the mutilation of the herms, led to the impiety charge against Alcibiades.

14. The involvement of men of means is confirmed by the surviving fragments recording the sale by public auction of some of the confiscated property; the fullest analysis of the material is W. K. Pritchett, "The Attic Stelai," *Hesperia,* 22 (1953) 225–99; 25 (1956) 178–328.

15. *Dissertations and Discussions* [1:30], vol. 2, 540.

16. The fullest account remains Paul Cloché, *La Restauration démocratique à Athènes en 403 avant J.-C.* (Paris 1915); cf. A. P. Dorjahn, *Political Forgiveness in Old Athens* (Evanston, Ill., 1946); ed. Lévy, *Athènes devant la défaite de 404 (Bibli. des Ecoles françaises d'Athènes et Rome,* vol. 225, 1976).

17. What follows is essentially the analysis of the trial of Socrates I offered in my *Aspects of Antiquity* (2nd ed., Penguin 1977), ch. 5.

18. Xenophon, *Memorabilia,* 1.1.1; Diogenes Laertius, *Lives of the Philosophers,* 2.40. The latter quotes a certain Favorinus (early second century A.D.) as saying that the text was still available in the official Athenian archive, the Metroön, and there is nothing implausible about that. For a close (nonjuristic) analysis of the wording, see Reginald Hackforth, *The Composition of Plato's Apology* (Cambridge 1933), ch. 4.

19. *The Open Society and Its Enemies* (4th ed., London 1962), vol. 1, 194.

CHAPTER 5

1. E. R. Dodds, *The Greeks and the Irrational* (Berkeley 1951), p.188.

2. Quoted from A. Harnack, *Geschichte der altchristlichen Literatur bis Eusebius*, Part 1 (Leipzig 1893), p. xxi.

3. A. F. Wert, cited by H. Bardon, *La littérature latine inconnue*, vol. 1 (Paris 1952), p. 13.

4. "The Collection of Genealogies," *Rhodes-Livingstone Journal*, 5 (1947) 48–55.

5. See A. D. E. Cameron, "Literary Allusions in the Historia Augusta," *Hermes*, 92 (1964) 363–77.

6. See F. H. Cramer, "Bookburning and Censorship in Ancient Rome," *Journal of the History of Ideas*, 6 (1945) 157–96; cf. W. Speyer, "Bücherverbrennung," in *Jahrbuch für Antike und Christentum*, 13 (1970) 123–52.

7. Harnack, *Geschichte der altchristlichen Literatur*, p. xxivn2.

8. H. D. Jocelyn, "The Poet Cn. Naevius, P. Cornelius Scipio and Q. Caecilius Metellus," *Antichthon*, 3 (1969) 32–47, at p. 34.

9. A. Momigliano, in *Dictionary of the History of Ideas*, vol. 2 (New York 1973), p. 261.

10. E. A. Havelock, *Preface to Plato* (Oxford 1963), p. 40.

11. Cicero, *Republic* 4.10.12; see J. A. Crook, *Law and Life at Rome* (London 1967), pp. 251–52.

12. H. D. Jocelyn, "The Ruling Class of the Roman Republic and Greek Philosophers," *Bulletin of the John Rylands Library*, 59 (1977) 323–66, at p. 359.

13. Suetonius, *De rhetoribus* 1–2, quoted from M. L. Clarke, *Rhetoric at Rome* (London 1953), pp. 11–12.

14. See F. H. Cramer, *Astrology in Roman Law and Politics* (Philadelphia 1954). On the formal and legal aspects,

Cramer has been corrected by R. A. Bauman, *Impietas in principem* (Munich 1974), esp. pp. 59–69.

15. Cramer, *Astrology in Roman Law and Politics*, p. 247.

16. See W. S. Ferguson, *Hellenistic Athens* (London 1911), pp. 104–7.

17. P. A. Brunt, "Stoicism and the Principate," *Papers of the British School at Rome*, 43 (1975) 7–35, at p. 10.

18. Dodds, *Greeks and the Irrational*, pp. 243–44.

Index

Academy of Plato, 134, 168
Acharnians (Aristophanes), 53, 119, 182n10
Acropolis in Athens, 86
Acton, John Dalberg-Acton, Lord, 74
Aeschines, 152
Aeschylus, 47
Alcibiades, 43; expedition against Sicily and, 39, 40, 58, 65; flight to Sparta, 126; recall of, 126–127; trial for impiety, 125–126, 183n13
Alexander the Great, 65, 140, 169
Alien and Sedition Acts (U.S., 1798), 114
American Revolution, 10
Anaxagoras of Clazomenae, 123, 136–137
Anytus, 73, 158, 161, 163; Socrates and, 64, 129, 132–133, 134, 138
Apathy (political), 3, 4, 12, 30, 36, 173n6
Apology (Plato), 139. *See also* Socrates, trial of
Apology (Xenophon), 130
Aristophanes, 42, 75, 150, 171, 177n4; anti-intellectualism and, 124; jokes of, 120,

136, 181n25, 182n10; political dissent and, 53, 119–121, 135; Socrates' trial and, 133
Aristotle, 5, 41–42, 63, 68; on community, 29, 30, 90–91; on faction (*stasis*), 47; on Pericles, 68; on popular rule, 4, 13, 17, 19–20, 47–48, 50; on slavery, 15–16, 104
Athenian court system, 116–119
Augustus, 151

Bacchus, cult of, 164, 166
Bachrach, Peter, on elitism, 176n40
Barnes, John, 148
Bell, Daniel, on consensus, 180n19
Berlin, Sir Isaiah, on coercion, 6
Bismarck, Otto von, 91
Britain: decision on joining Common Market, 98–99; elitism and, 9, 35, 36n
Brunt, P. A., 170
Brutus, 147
Byzantium, 172

Caligula, 147
Cantril, Hadley, on ideology, 181n28

Capitalism, Socialism and Democracy (Schumpeter), 5, 176n33
Carneades, 159
Cassius, 147
Cato, 159, 160, 161, 162–163
Christians, 166, 169
Cicero, 149, 152, 153, 162
Cimon, 68
Claudius, 145
Cleon, 42, 43, 53, 59, 63, 73; Aristophanes and, 120–121; policy of frightfulness and, 55
Cleophon, 73
Clisthenes, 66
Clouds (Aristophanes), 124, 133, 144
Columbus, Christopher, 14
Constitution of Athens (Aristotle), 30, 63
Constitution of Athens (Ps.Xenophon), 23
Cremutius Cordus, 147, 148–149

Damonides, pay for jurors and, 68
Decius, 166
DeGaulle, Charles, on national duties, 90
Demagogues, 41–44, 177n4
Democracy (Jones), 179n23
Democratic Elitism (Bachrach), 176n40
Demosthenes, 75, 152
de Ste. Croix, 182n25
Dio Cassius, 168
Diocletian, 166
Diogenes Laertius, 156, 183n18
Dionysus, 121
Diopeithes, anti-impiety law of, 122–123, 129, 136–139

Dodds, E. R., 144, 172
Dover, K. J., on Aristophanes, 181n25

Ehrenberg, 50, 179n20
Elitism, 7–11, 15, 19–20, 24–25, 33, 36–37
End of Ideology, The (Bell), 180n19
Ephialtes, 41–42, 107
Epicurus, 169
Eratosthenes, 172
Eumenides, 47
Euripides, 154, 156
Exile, 134, 146, 155, 158, 162, 163, 167

France, 9–10, 78
Free, L. A., on ideology, 181n28
French Revolution, 9–10
Funeral Oration (Pericles), 30

Gellius, 150
General Motors Corporation, 38, 76
Genovese, Eugene, 103
Germany, 8, 80
Gomme, A. W., 177n3
Gramsci, Antonio, 103
Greek armed forces, 83
Greek maritime states, league of, 81–82
Greek religion, 115–116
Greenland Eskimos, 105
Grimond, Jo, on state institutions, 122
Grote, George, 38–39, 62

Harnack, 149
Havelock, Eric, 49, 156
Hegel, Georg Wilhelm Friedrich, 170–171

Historical Commentary on Thucydides (Gomme), 177*n*3
Hogg, Quintin, on Aristophanes, 183*n*10
Hume, David, 70, 71

Iliad (Homer), 113
Isocrates, 153
Italy, 7–8, 78

Jakobsen, Thorkild, on obedience in Mesopotamia, 113
Jews, 166
Jones, A. H. M., 49–50, 179*n*23
Jones, Frank, 157
Jones, Morris, 106
Julian, 169
Jury service, 20, 68, 117–119
Justinian, 169
Juvenal, 148

Kakodaimonistai (devil worshipers), 139
Kissinger, Henry: on bureaucracy, 98; on leadership, 34–36, 176*n*35
Knights (Aristophanes), 183*n*10

Laws (Plato), 135
Leach, Sir Edmund, 143
Leadership, 40–43
Lipset, Seymour Martin, 5; elitism and, 4, 6–7, 8; on fantasies, 106
Lives of the Philosophers (Diogenes Laertius), 183*n*18
Livy, 165
Loenen, D., 177*n*5
Long, Huey, 10
Louis XIV, king of France, 80

Lycon, 129
Lysistrata (Aristophanes), 119, 183*n*10

McCallum, R. B., 60
McCarthy, Joseph, 10
Mann, Michael, 28
Marcus Aurelius, 169
Marxists, 103–105
Meinecke, Friedrich, on *Staatsräson*, 89–91
Meletus, 129, 130, 134
Meno (Plato), 132, 158
Mesopotamia, 14, 113
Meynaud, Jean, 175*n*20
Michels, Robert, 9, 14, 16–17
Miliband, Ralph, 176*n*37
Mill, John Stuart: on democratic education, 31–32; on law and individual liberty, 110–111, 112; on the Thirty Tyrants, 128
Momigliana, A., 49, 153
Morris Jones, W. H., 4, 5
Mosca, Gaetano, 7, 174*n*15
Mussolini, Benito, 8, 11
Mytilene, 55

Naevius, 150, 152
Nero, 166
Nicias, General, 40; expedition against Sicily and, 39, 58
Nicias (Plutarch), 154

Odysseus, 113
Oedipus (Sophocles), 167
On the Nature of the Gods (Cicero), 155
Open Society and Its Enemies (Popper), 6
Ostracism, 26, 72, 113
Ovid, 148

Palmer, Robert R., on the
   philosophes, 9–10
Panaetius of Rhodes, 170
Pareto, Vilfredo, 7
Parry, Geraint: on language, 9;
   on Schumpeter, 5–6
*Participation and Democracy
   Theory* (Pateman), 176n40
Partridge, P. L., 99, 100
Pateman, Carole, 176n40
Peace (Aristophanes), 136,
   183n10
Peloponnesian War, 26, 59, 64,
   81, 102; Aristophanes and,
   119–121, 136; Athenian entry
   in, 25, 81; decision to
   engage in, 94–95; political
   criticism and, 135–136
Pericles, 23–24, 25, 30, 40, 66,
   73, 88, 97; death of, 63;
   deposed, 55
Persia, invasion of Greece, 81,
   93
Philip of Macedon, 93; Athenian
   war against, 81, 140
Piraeus of Athens, 17
Pisander, 56
Plato, 71, 75, 79, 155, 161, 163,
   169; Academy of, 134, 168;
   on education, 20, 30;
   opposition to open society,
   134–135, 153, 158; on political
   good, 4, 5, 6, 7, 47; Socrates'
   trial and, 130–134; Sophists
   and, 28–29
Plutarch, 154
Political Beliefs (Free and
   Cantril), 181n28
Political Parties (Michels), 7–8
Politics (Aristotle), 4, 13, 15, 17,
   19, 47, 50
Popper, Sir Karl, 6

Protagoras, 156; democratic
   theory and, 28–29, 79, 132;
   education in, 30, 31; exile of,
   155, 162
Protagorus (Plato), 28
Pseudo-Xenophon, on
   democracy, 23, 88
Public funds, distribution of,
   86–87

Quintilian, 147
Quislings, 93

Republic (Plato), 46, 158
Rome, ancient, 14n, 34

Schumpeter, Joseph, 5–6,
   175n26, 176n33; on
   leadership, 24
Seneca, 151
Sicily, Athenian invasion of,
   20–23, 31, 33, 95
Socrates, 28, 31, 161; trial of,
   117, 118, 123, 128–135,
   136–37
Solon, 30
Sophists, 28–29, 158; diatribe
   against, 161; education and,
   30, 31, 131–132, 133, 139
Sophocles, 167
Sparta, 25, 81; Athen's war
   with, 114
Staatsräson, 89–91
Stasis (Loenen), 177n5
Stoics, 169, 170
Suetonius, 145, 151, 160–161
Suppliant Women (Euripides),
   156
Switzerland, 175n26
Syracuse, 154–155

Tacitus, 147, 151
Taxes, 83–84

Theocritus, 172

Thersites, 113

Thirty Tyrants, 139; overthrow of, 73, 128

Thrasybulus, 73

Thrasymachus: on political ethics, 79, 89

Thucydides, 42–43, 55–56, 71, 167; on democracy and leaders, 40–41, 47; on Pericles, 24, 25, 30; on Sicilian expedition, 20–22, 38, 39, 66, 95

Tiresias, 167

Tocqueville, Alexis de, 32, 33

Vlastos, G., 73

Wahlke, J. C., 173n6

Wasps (Aristophanes), 183n10

Wordsworth, William, 10

Xenophon, 63–64, 71; Socrates' trial and, 130–131, 134